MOVIE
RECORD BREAKERS

The biggest, the baddest and the best movies of all time!

MOVIE
RECORD BREAKERS

The biggest, the baddest and the best movies of all time!

DAVID BARRACLOUGH

CHARTWELL
BOOKS, INC.

To Sarah and Michael, despite their
moving on FA Cup Final Day.

A QUINTET BOOK

Published by Chartwell Books
A Division of Book Sales, Inc.
110 Enterprise Avenue
Secaucus, New Jersey 07094

This edition produced for sale
in the U.S.A., its territories
and dependencies only.

ISBN 1-55521-771-0

This book was designed and produced by
Quintet Publishing Limited
6 Blundell Street
London N7 9BH

Project Editor: Laura Sandelson
Creative Director: Richard Dewing
Designer: Chris Dymond
Editor: Rosemary Booton

Typeset in Great Britain by
Central Southern Typesetters, Eastbourne
Manufactured in Hong Kong by Regent Publishing Services Limited
Printed in Hong Kong by Leefung-Asco Printers Limited

ACKNOWLEDGEMENTS

Special thanks to Helen Burke for her invaluable help and advice
during the preparation of the manuscript, to Simon Bebbington for
his many useful suggestions, to Leigh Baulch, Bob Kelly, Viv Mager
and Katy Wild for digging into their video collections, and to Bobby
Valentino, Barry Adamson and Primal Scream for providing the
perfect soundtrack.

The publishers would like to extend special thanks to the Joel
Finler Collection for providing the majority of the pictures featured
in this book.

NOTE

All financial tables, unless otherwise stated, are taken from the
invaluable American publication *Variety*. Box office figures are for
American and Canadian cinemas only, up to December 1990.
Since *Variety* includes reissue figures for these movies, it should
be noted that not every film in their listing of box office winners
proved a massive hit on initial releases. The Disney cartoons are
an obvious example.

CONTENTS

The Money

BIGGEST MONEY-MAKERS

David Wark Griffith is generally considered American silent cinema's leading figure, often credited with popularizing, if not actually inventing, many film-making techniques now considered standard. His influence was felt at the box-office too, where three of his movies took over $3 million (as opposed, for example, to only one of Chaplin's). Towering over all his movies is *The Birth of a Nation*, an epic American Civil War saga based on Thomas Dixon Jnr's racist novel *The Klansman*.

Featured behind the camera was an impressive array of talent: future directors Erich Von Stroheim, Jack Conway, Victor Fleming and Raoul Walsh, plus the cinema's first great cameraman and Griffith's regular partner for 16 years, Billy Bitzer. The film starred Griffith regulars Lillian Gish, H B

RIGHT Colonel Ben Cameron (Henry B Walthall) and Flora Cameron (Mae Marsh) in *The Birth of a Nation*.

RIGHT *The Birth of a Nation* helped inspire the rebirth of the Ku-Klux-Klan.

Walthall and Mae Marsh, while also in the cast were Elmo Lincoln, the cinema's first Tarzan, regular Laurel and Hardy villain Walter Long, silent stars Bessie Love and Wallace Reid, and later leading character actor Eugene Pallette. Nevertheless, at a cost of $100,000, it was confidently predicted by many that the film could never hope to recoup its budget.

The Birth of a Nation, based on a highly sensitive war still within living memory, reopened old wounds and was released in a storm of controversy, particularly because of its depiction of the Ku-Klux-Klan as heroes. It was obviously a genuinely important subject to Griffith, who came from the South, had previously covered this period in *The Battle* (1911) and seems to have been surprised by the ensuing criticism. Compared with its source, *The Birth of a Nation* was relatively mild. The reaction spurred Griffith to defend himself in a pamphlet entitled "The Rise and Fall of Free Speech in America". Still, he was hardly unaware of the beneficial effects such controversy might have on the box-office takings, saying "I hope to God they do stop it [ban the picture]. Then you won't be able to keep the audiences away with clubs". And they couldn't. It opened at the Liberty in New York and ran for 44 weeks.

ALL-TIME BOX-OFFICE HITS

		DIRECTOR	DATE	TOTAL RENTALS
1	ET THE EXTRA-TERRESTRIAL	SPIELBERG	1982	228,618,939
2	STAR WARS	LUCAS	1977	193,500,000
3	RETURN OF THE JEDI	MARQUAND	1983	168,002,414
4	BATMAN	BURTON	1989	150,500,000
5	THE EMPIRE STRIKES BACK	KERSHNER	1980	141,600,000
6	GHOSTBUSTERS	REITMAN	1984	132,720,000
7	JAWS	SPIELBERG	1975	129,549,325
8	RAIDERS OF THE LOST ARK	SPIELBERG	1981	115,598,000
9	INDIANA JONES AND THE LAST CRUSADE	SPIELBERG	1989	115,500,000
10	INDIANA JONES AND THE TEMPLE OF DOOM	SPIELBERG	1984	109,000,000

LEFT "In the year 2024 the most important single thing which the cinema will have helped in a large way to accomplish will be that of eliminating from the face of the civilized world all armed conflict," wrote Griffith in 1924.

The criticism it has received is not unwarranted. *The Birth of a Nation* may, for the period, be technically impressive, but it is also highly racist. However, banning the film, then as now, was not the solution – the protestors' cause was hardly helped by many not having actually seen the film. Surprisingly, it initially received praise from President Woodrow Wilson, who said "It is like writing history with lightning", although he later had to withdraw his support. Less surprisingly, it attracted glowing reviews, such as the *New York Globe*'s "beyond doubt the most extraordinary picture that has been seen".

Even the glowing reviews can't hide the fact that the film was highly influential in the revival of the Ku-Klux-Klan, which had disbanded in 1869. By the mid-twenties its membership had grown to 4,000,000. Yet *The Birth of a Nation* remains an

BELOW "The high point of my career." John Gilbert (centre) in King Vidor's *The Big Parade*.

important achievement, if only for demonstrating the power of the cinema and proving that an expensive feature film could be a commercial success. The other two Griffith hits, both using the talents of Gish and Bitzer, were less influential: *Hearts of the World* is a First World War movie featuring the Gish sisters, Erich Von Stroheim and Noel Coward, while *Way Down East* is an old-fashioned melodrama, in which an innocent woman is deserted by her wicked husband once she becomes pregnant, for which Griffith paid a then-record $175,000 to acquire the rights. It is still an effective film, particularly during the memorable climactic ice-floe sequence.

The best of the remaining ten is King Vidor's classic war movie *The Big Parade*, which confirmed John Gilbert (whom

RIGHT Lillian Gish and Richard Barthelmess in *Way Down East* for which Griffith paid a then record of $175,000 to acquire the rights.

ADOLPH ZUKOR and JESSE L LASKY
present
THE
MIGHTIEST
DRAMATIC
SPECTACLE
OF ALL THE
AGES

"The TEN COMMANDMENTS"

BY
CECIL B.
DeMILLE

Story by Jeanie Macpherson.
PRODUCTION OF THE
FAMOUS PLAYERS
LASKY CORPORATION

A Paramount Production

RIGHT Cecil B DeMille's *The Ten Commandments* was later remade by DeMille and became the fifties' biggest box-office hit.

RIGHT *Ben Hur* was another great pre-thirties hit which cost a staggering $4 million.

The other hits include two movies that were remade to equal success in the fifties, *Ben Hur* and Cecil B DeMille's first attempt to film *The Ten Commandments*. Neither movie had trouble-free productions. After three months filming, Louis B Mayer and Irving Thalberg were unhappy with the *Ben Hur* rushes, replaced director Charles Brabin and star George Walsh with Fred Niblo and Roman Novarro, and later recalled the unit from Italy to complete the film in Hollywood. Three years earlier, DeMille had suffered increasing pressure from Paramount as the budget on *The Ten Commandments* escalated, prompting him to enquire: "Do they want me to quit now and release it as *The Five Commandments?*" He finally won the day, completing the movie at a cost of $1.5 million.

The remaining three films are: Al Jolson's part-talkie follow-up to *The Jazz Singer* (1927), *The Singing Fool*, an overly sentimental tale of a musician's fall after a bad marriage, before being rescued by the love of a good woman; *The Four Horsemen of the Apocalypse*, the film that made Rudolph Valentino a star; and the epic western *The Covered Wagon*, filmed by James Cruze who by 1927 was Hollywood's highest-paid director.

Vidor had initially not wanted to use) as a star after his performance in Von Stroheim's *The Merry Widow* earlier the same year. It also elevated Vidor's status, opening to uniformly fine reviews and running at New York's Astor Cinema for 96 weeks. Years later Vidor seemed disappointed with the results: "Today I don't encourage people to see the film. At the time I really believed it was an anti-war movie." This was not quite his idea when production started: "I do not wish to appear to be taking a stand about war. I certainly do not favor it, but I would not set up a preachment against it." Despite Vidor's later claims, it remains both a fine war movie and a first-rate love story. It's certainly more interesting than the other hit war movie, Raoul Walsh's *What Price Glory?*, which starred Victor McLaglen and Edmund Lowe as Captain Flagg and Sergeant Quirt.

ABOVE Location filming of James Cruze's 1923 western hit *The Covered Wagon*, based on a *Saturday Evening Post* serial.

BOX-OFFICE HITS OF THE PRE-THIRTIES

		DIRECTOR	DATE	TOTAL RENTALS
1	THE BIRTH OF A NATION	GRIFFITH	1915	10,000,000
2	THE BIG PARADE	VIDOR	1925	5,120,791
3	BEN HUR	NIBLO	1926	4,578,634
4	THE TEN COMMANDMENTS	DeMILLE	1923	4,100,000
5	THE COVERED WAGON	CRUZE	1923	4,000,000
	WHAT PRICE GLORY?	WALSH	1926	4,000,000
7	HEARTS OF THE WORLD	GRIFFITH	1918	3,900,000
	WAY DOWN EAST	GRIFFITH	1920	3,900,000
9	THE SINGING FOOL	BACON	1928	3,821,000
10	THE FOUR HORSEMEN OF THE APOCALYPSE	INGRAM	1921	3,800,000

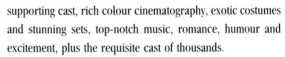

BOX-OFFICE HITS OF THE THIRTIES

	DIRECTOR	DATE	TOTAL RENTALS
1 GONE WITH THE WIND	FLEMING	1939	79,375,077
2 SNOW WHITE AND THE SEVEN DWARFS	HAND	1937	61,752,000
3 FANTASIA	SHARPSTEEN	1940	41,660,000
4 PINOCCHIO	SHARPSTEEN/LUSKE	1940	32,957,000
5 KING KONG	COOPER/SCHOEDSACK	1933	5,000,000
6 THE WIZARD OF OZ	FLEMING	1939	4,759,888
7 BOOM TOWN	CONWAY	1940	4,586,415
8 SAN FRANCISCO	VAN DYKE	1936	3,785,868
9 LOST HORIZON	CAPRA	1937	3,500,000
MR SMITH GOES TO WASHINGTON	CAPRA	1939	3,500,000

BELOW "I haven't the slightest intention of playing another weak, watery character such as Ashley Wilkes," said Leslie Howard. Leslie Howard as Ashley Wilkes, with Vivien Leigh and Olivia de Haviland in *Gone with the Wind.*

Walt Disney, Clark Gable and Frank Capra dominate the box-office hits of the thirties, the decade that produced the finest commercial successes. In *Gone with the Wind*, which is probably the most widely seen movie, it certainly produced the most enduring success. This film was reissued for each new generation who were eager to see it. Given its confusing production – using a multitude of writers, with directors resigning and the late casting of the central role of Scarlett O'Hara – for a while the success of *Gone with the Wind* must have seemed doubtful. But it is now considered the embodiment of "Golden Age Hollywood": glamorous stars, excellent supporting cast, rich colour cinematography, exotic costumes and stunning sets, top-notch music, romance, humour and excitement, plus the requisite cast of thousands.

In the summer of 1936 Margaret Mitchell's novel, which took her 10 years to write, was already a massive bestseller and was suggested as a possible project for Selznick. However, his story editor, Val Lewton – later a noted producer himself – disliked the novel, considering it trash. And Selznick felt it was too long. In fact, he might never have made the movie had not John Hay Whitney, the Selznick International board chairman, offered to buy the rights himself. This spurred Selznick into action.

George Cukor, who had worked with Selznick on five previous occasions, was assigned as director, and playwright Sidney Howard was hired to write the script. But most attention was given to the casting of Scarlett O'Hara. The quest dominated the pages of fan magazines and led to three talent searches in the Southern states, with numerous actresses being screen-tested for the role, including Lana Turner, Paulette Goddard (who was at one time Selznick's favourite for the part) and Jean Arthur. The perfect Scarlett was finally found in British actress Vivien Leigh, who claimed to feel an affinity with the part and was finally cast on Christmas Day 1938, after the burning of Atlanta had been shot. She had, in fact, been recommended as early as February 1937 by one of Selznick's own scouts.

TIME
THE WEEKLY NEWSMAGAZINE

SCARLETT O'HARA
To Dave & Myron, Vivien Leigh.
(Cinema)

The casting of the other roles might have seemed simple by comparison, but were not without their headaches. The public would accept only one person as Rhett Butler – Clark Gable. This presented Selznick with two problems. Firstly, Gable wasn't keen on accepting the role, not wanting another historical part after the box-office failure of *Parnell* (1937) as well as feeling "too many people know this character". Complicating the problem further, Gable was under contract to MGM. An agreement was finally reached on 24 August 1938, in which MGM would provide Gable and half the budget up to a maximum of $1.25 million in return for worldwide distribution rights and half the profits for seven years.

Leslie Howard also needed persuading to take the role of Ashley Wilkes ("I've played enough ineffectual characters already"), only accepting in return for the opportunity to produce and star in *Intermezzo* (1939; *Escape to Happiness*).

LEFT The search for Scarlett O'Hara and Vivien Leigh's ensuing success from the role provided great publicity for her, featuring on numerous magazine covers.

BELOW *Gone with the Wind* made over $6 million on both its 1961 and 1967 American reissues.

Olivia de Havilland was always first choice to play Melanie, but was under contract to Warner Brothers at the time and had to plead with them to be allowed to take the role. Also, during this time, the script went through many rewrites, some work being undertaken by F Scott Fitzgerald, all under the close supervision of Selznick.

On 26 January 1939 principal photography commenced, but the film soon ran into trouble. The rushes were unsatisfactory, Cukor blaming this on what he considered a poor script. He left the film to be replaced by Victor Fleming, whom MGM took off *The Wizard of Oz*. There followed 17 days of further rewrites, this time by Ben Hecht. Filming recommenced on 2 March, but Selznick was still not happy with the results. This time it was the turn of cinematographer Lee Garmes to leave. His replacement was Ernest Haller, who had shot Warner Brothers' Civil War melodrama *Jezebel*

BELOW *Gone with the Wind*'s 10 Oscars was a record in 1939. Vivien Leigh was named Best Actress, but Clark Gable lost out.

(1938) the previous year. The film went over budget, Sidney Howard was brought back for yet more rewrites and an exhausted Victor Fleming was replaced by Sam Wood for two weeks, before the film was completed using both directors.

But still the hard work continued. First there were retakes, followed by four months of editing. Thankfully, the results justified the painstaking work all round, and the first sneak preview, on 9 September, was a resounding success. But there was still the music to be scored, as well as the struggle to get the then censurable line "Frankly my dear, I don't give a damn" past the censors.

All was finally completed for the world premiere in Atlanta, Georgia on 15 December 1939, for which the star-studded cast turned out. Further celebrations followed on 29 February 1940, Oscar night, when *Gone with the Wind* swept the awards, with only Clark Gable losing out to Robert Donat in *Goodbye*

December 1937, at the Carthay Circle Theater in Los Angeles, it has been a great success, which was fortunate for Disney as the film had taken 750 artists over three years to complete at a cost of $1.5 million. Perhaps not ranking among Disney's very best – the romantic leads, Snow White and the Prince, are rather dull – it does boast a strong villain in the wicked Queen and great comic support from the seven dwarfs (Doc, Dopey, Grumpy, Happy, Bashful, Sleepy and Sneezy) who together sing the movie's two best songs, "Whistle While You Work" and "Heigh Ho".

LEFT *The Wizard of Oz* featured Munchkins, talking trees, monkeys, men made of tin and straw, cowardly lions and a dog called Toto, together making the film a great success.

BELOW *The Wizard of Oz* proved a huge hit for MGM, although in Britain it was considered suitable for adults only.

Mr Chips (1939). Unfortunately, Sidney Howard, who was among the Oscar winners, died in an accident before he saw the completed film.

Two other Gable films made the top ten (*Boom Town* and *San Francisco*, both co-starring Spencer Tracy), but are relatively uninteresting in comparison with the other money-makers of the period. MGM, which produced both these Gable movies, had another huge hit with the perennial favourite *The Wizard of Oz*, featuring Munchkins, talking trees, flying monkeys, men made of tin and straw, cowardly lions and a dog called Toto. It is a wonderful film, with some fine songs (although "Over the Rainbow" was very nearly cut), superb performances, great characters, imaginative sets and a strong story, deftly mixing humour and a storyline that was frightening in parts. All this to prove there's no place like home, except, perhaps, the Emerald City and the merry old land of Oz. It might have been a little different if MGM had secured Shirley Temple for the part of Dorothy (rather than Judy Garland) as they had originally intended.

Oz had its problems too. On its British release, Graham Greene wrote: "The British Board of Film Censors have given this picture a certificate for adults only. Surely it is time that this absurd committee of elderly men and spinsters who feared, too, that *Snow White* was unsuitable for those under sixteen, was laughed out of existence." It is funny how some things never change.

The aforementioned *Snow White and the Seven Dwarfs* is one of three Disney films in the top 10 and was also the Studio's first animated feature. Ever since its premiere on 21

There are no such reservations about the quality of
Pinocchio, Disney's second animated feature. It tells the story
of woodcutter Geppetto and the puppet he creates, which is
given life by the Blue Fairy. She promises to make the puppet
Pinocchio real if he proves himself to be honest and brave.
There are some memorable supporting characters – Jiminy
Cricket, Foulfellow and his sidekick Gideon the cat, Monstro
the whale and Figaro the cat – and popular songs like "There
are No Strings On Me" and "When You Wish Upon a Star",
the latter winning an Oscar. *Pinocchio* cost $2.6 million to
produce and on its original release lost $1 million. By which
time *Fantasia* had been released, costing even more at $3
million. This uneven film took eight pieces of classical music
conducted by Leopold Stokowski and set animation to them.
The animation is fine, but there are some overly cute sequences,
for example the appearance of Cupid during the "Pastoral

KING KONG

FAY WRAY
ROB'T ARMSTRONG
BRUCE CABOT

A PERSONALLY DIRECTED
MERIAN C.

Symphony", and *Fantasia* hardly ranks as one of Disney's artistic successes, although naturally it has its defenders.

The remaining films are two Frank Capra movies, *Lost Horizon* and *Mr Smith Goes to Washington*, and *King Kong*. *Kong* is still one of the finest monster movies, if not *the* finest, the world of Skull Island and the special effects remaining convincing nearly 60 years after its production. It is vastly preferable to the expensive remake or, indeed, its own cut-price sequel. *Lost Horizon* also ventures into the fantastic – to the magical world of Shangri-La. Not absolutely top-notch Capra, particularly since it followed close on the heels of *It Happened One Night* (1934) and *Mr Deeds Goes to Town* (1936), but it does feature the expected fine cast (Colman,

Mitchell, Horton, Jaffe) and Robert Conway is a typically idealistic Capra hero. Sadly, it too suffered the indignity of a dreadful remake.

Mr Smith Goes to Washington is certainly the better of the Capra movies. Idealistic, naïve everyman Jefferson Smith is the perfect James Stewart role (although Gary Cooper was Capra's first choice), and there are equally ideal parts for Jean Arthur, Claude Rains, Thomas Mitchell, Edward Arnold, Guy Kibbee, Eugene Pallette and a host of splendid Hollywood supporting actors. This tale of idealism and democracy, as innocent Smith stands up against corrupt politicians, seemed particularly timely on its release in October 1939. But, again, there was another abysmal remake.

BELOW Jefferson Smith believes in "one simple plain truth. Love thy neighbour". Guy Kibbee, James Stewart and Beulah Bondi seen in Frank Capra's *Mr Smith Goes to Washington*.

BOX-OFFICE HITS OF THE FORTIES

		DIRECTOR	DATE	TOTAL RENTALS
1	BAMBI	HAND	1942	47,265,000
2	CINDERELLA	JACKSON/LUSKE/ GERONIMI	1950	41,087,000
3	SONG OF THE SOUTH	FOSTER	1946	29,228,717
4	MOM AND DAD	BEAUDINE	1944	16,000,000
5	SAMSON AND DELILAH	DeMILLE	1949	11,500,000
6	THE BEST YEARS OF OUR LIVES	WYLER	1946	11,300,000
	DUEL IN THE SUN	VIDOR	1946	11,300,000
8	THIS IS THE ARMY	CURTIZ	1943	8,500,000
9	THE BELLS OF ST MARY'S	McCAREY	1945	8,000,000
10	THE JOLSON STORY	GREEN	1946	7,600,000

Disney cartoons, because of their continuing appeal and constant reissues, occupy the top three spots, although surprisingly there's no place for *Dumbo* (1941). Disney aside, the forties offered an interesting variety of hits, from flag-waving musicals to serious dramas, from religious epics to low-budget exploitation movies.

Bambi is the best of the three Disney movies and, with over $47 million to its credit by 1990, the most successful. It was the last of a classic quartet – *Pinocchio* (1940), *Fantasia*

RIGHT "The most honoured picture of our time!" William Wyler's *The Best Years of Our Lives* was named Best Picture at the Academy Awards, the New York Film Critics Awards and the Golden Globe Awards and was featured on both *The New York Times'* and *Time* magazine's 1946 "Ten Best" list.

(1940) and *Dumbo* are the other three – released over a three-year period between 1940 and 1942. The rather low-key story concentrates on Bambi's coming of age, illustrated through the changing seasons and the use of four different voices for the Bambi character. Although a slight departure from much of Disney's work, in that it has less of a strong narrative and attempts a more naturalistic style of animation, it ranks among the Studio's best work.

Bambi was the last animated feature to be released until *Cinderella* in 1950. There were problems at the Disney Studio: the 1941 strike over pay and unionization led to the loss of some of Disney's finest animators, and the war also claimed some talented employees, as well as creating financial problems by obviously reducing the overseas market. After such a long interval without animation, *Cinderella* was a disappointment, with dull human characters, although Lucifer the cat and the mice, Jacques and Gus, are enjoyable. The third Disney movie, *Song of the South*, mixed animation with live action, as Uncle Remus told stories of Brer Rabbit, Brer Bear and Brer Fox. The animation was excellent, much better than the live-action sequences, and the film did feature the popular, Oscar-winning song "Zip-a-Dee-Do-Dah", but *Song of the South* was still some way behind *Pinocchio, Dumbo* and *Bambi*.

Alongside *Bambi*, the best film in the top 10 is William Wyler's *The Best Years of Our Lives*, which tells of three servicemen (Dana Andrews, Fredric March and Harold Russell)

returning home after the Second World War and their problems readjusting to home life and routine jobs. The story is based on actual cases. "This is not a story of plot, but a picture of some people, who were real people, facing real problems," said Wyler. It is difficult to find fault with this Sam Goldwyn production, which in 1946 must have seemed refreshingly forthright about the problems facing war veterans. *The Best Years of Our Lives* brought Oscars for Robert Sherwood's first-rate script, Hugo Friedhofer's music, Daniel Mandell's editing, Fredric March's and Harold Russell's performances and, inevitably, Wyler's direction. Harold Russell, a real-life handicapped veteran who didn't appear in another

movie until 1980's *Inside Moves*, also won a Special Oscar and the film was judged Best Picture. Incredibly, Gregg Toland's wonderful cinematography was overlooked, while Dana Andrews never seems to have got the credit he deserves. Also outstanding in the cast were Myrna Loy as March's wife and Hoagy Carmichael playing, well, Hoagy Carmichael.

The other successes of the forties were producer David O Selznick's attempt to repeat the success of *Gone with the Wind* (1939) with the full-blooded western melodrama *Duel in the Sun*, which starred Gregory Peck, Selznick's wife Jennifer Jones, Joseph Cotten, Lionel Barrymore, Lillian Gish and Walter Huston. It turned out to be a really profitable movie

BELOW Harold Russell, Teresa Wright, Dana Andrews, Myrna Loy and Fredric March in *The Best Years of Our Lives.*

RIGHT "You can say that I'm lavish, but you can't say that I'm wasteful." Cecil B DeMille's epic *Samson and Delilah*, starring Hedy Lamarr and Victor Mature.

played, helped in no small part by the flamboyant Babb, and produced huge queues at the box-office. The threatened law suits and talk of obscenity charges were great publicity for Babb. He whipped up further interest by insisting on sexually segregated showing (an old, yet effective gimmick) and made further profit by hiring a lecturer (always named Elliott Forbes) to sell sex hygiene books during an intermission, backed up by assistants in nurses' uniforms. No one ever questioned how it was possible for Elliott Forbes to lecture in up to 25 places at once, but then they were probably too busy enjoying Babb's hard-sell advertising techniques. They paid handsome dividends.

LEFT Larry Parks imitating Al Jolson in *The Jolson Story.* **Its success led to** *Jolson Sings Again* **(1949).**

despite its delays in production and escalating costs. Selznick went on to make other films but never managed to repeat his earlier successes. Other hits of the forties were Warner Brothers' patriotic musical *This is the Army*, starring the dull George Murphy and Joan Leslie, and featuring songs by Irving Berlin, with all the profits going to the Army Emergency Relief; the Cecil B DeMille religious epic *Samson and Delilah*, with Victor Mature and Hedy Lamarr in the title roles, which caused one critic to comment "Samson got shorn, but the Bible got scalped"; the sanitized and unexciting musical biopic *The Jolson Story*, with Larry Parks doing the acting and Al Jolson providing the singing; and Bing Crosby's sequel to the hugely successful *Going My Way* (1944; 12th most successful film of the forties), *The Bells of St Mary's*, which again mixed religion, sentiment, children and Crosby's crooning, but this time replaced Barry Fitzgerald's ageing priest with Ingrid Bergman's Mother Superior. It was RKO's biggest hit.

The least publicized of all the top ten is *Mom and Dad*, presented for Hygienic Productions by the great showman Kroger Babb and directed by notorious quickie-director William Beaudine, who also has *Black Market Babies* (1946), *Bela Lugosi Meets a Brooklyn Gorilla* (1952) and *Jesse James Meets Frankenstein's Daughter* (1965) to his credit. The story is an old chestnut: naïve girl gets pregnant, boyfriend is killed before they are married, sex education is advocated by a school teacher, girl reconciled with parents. Happy ending aside, it is almost the stuff of Victorian melodrama, but *Mom and Dad* nevertheless generated controversy wherever it

★ NOTABLE FIRST ★

The first public screening was held on 22 March 1895 when the brothers Auguste and Louis Lumière presented *La Sortie des Ouvriers de l'Usine Lumière* (1894) before a specially selected audience in Paris. On 28 December they gave the first screening for a paying audience, at the Grand Café on the Boulevard des Capucines, again in Paris. Entrance fee was one franc.

BOX-OFFICE HITS OF THE FIFTIES

		DIRECTOR	DATE	TOTAL RENTALS
1	THE TEN COMMANDMENTS	DeMILLE	1956	43,000,000
2	LADY AND THE TRAMP	LUSKE/GERONIMI/ JACKSON	1955	40,249,000
3	PETER PAN	LUSKE/GERONIMI/ JACKSON	1953	37,584,000
4	BEN HUR	WYLER	1959	36,992,088
5	AROUND THE WORLD IN EIGHTY DAYS	ANDERSON	1956	23,120,000
6	SLEEPING BEAUTY	GERONIMI	1959	21,998,000
7	THE SWISS FAMILY ROBINSON	ANNAKIN	1960	20,178,000
8	THE ROBE	KOSTER	1953	17,500,000
	SOUTH PACIFIC	LOGAN	1958	17,500,000
10	BRIDGE ON THE RIVER KWAI	LEAN	1957	17,195,000

RIGHT David Lean was named Best Director, Alec Guinness Best Actor and *The Bridge on the River Kwai* Best Picture at the 1957 Academy Awards.

The fifties box-office hits are dominated by the Disney animated feature and the epic, be it religious, musical, war or adventure. The former owe their commercial success to their longevity, the timeless quality that enables Disney cartoons to be released anew for each generation. The epics, on the other hand, were produced partly in reaction to television's increasing popularity, providing a spectacle not available (for free) in the home. Many gimmicks, such as 3-D or William Castle's Emergo, which involved dangling a skeleton over the audience's heads, Percepto, which involved wiring up certain seats to provide a slight electric shock, *et al*, were tried to entice cinema-goers back to the movies. The most successful were Cinemascope, casts of thousands, an increasing use of colour and endless exotic locations. The undoubted master here was Cecil B DeMille, the king of the religious epic, who scored his greatest success with a remake of his silent hit *The Ten Commandments*. It was his last film as director, a movie (by his standards at least) impossible to top.

DeMille was a giant of the film industry, and his 1913 production *The Squaw Man* was frequently credited as the first major Hollywood movie. He gained immense popularity during the silent era with his *risqué* sex comedies and religious epics, the latter becoming his trademark for the remainder of his career. He did everything on a grand scale, even to the spelling of his name – the rest of his family were *de*Mille. But despite his commercial successes, the critics were less than kind. Witness the rhyme popular at Paramount:

"Cecil B DeMille
Much against his will
Was persuaded to keep Moses
Out of the War of the Roses."

Or, more specifically, the *Time* film critic on *The Ten Commandments*: "It is difficult to find another instance in which so large a golden calf has been set up without objection from religious leaders. With insuperable piety, Cinemogul DeMille claims that he has tried 'to translate the Bible back to its original form', the form in which it was lived. Yet what he has really done is to throw sex and sand into the movie-goers' eyes for almost twice as long as anybody else has ever dared to." This was criticism DeMille wasn't immune to, defensively claiming: "I win *my* awards at the box office." In the case of *The Ten Commandments* he was probably right, although the film did also receive an Oscar nomination for Best Picture.

DeMille also had a reputation for being an old-style film director, a dictatorial tyrant who could be hard on the many extras employed on his films, as Vincent Price (who acted in *The Ten Commandments*) hinted: "It was during the making of *The Ten Commandments* that the joke about the disenchanted woman extra was first heard: 'Who do you have to sleep with to get *off* this picture?'" Nevertheless, not many stars would have turned down a DeMille film. As Charlton Heston said: "If you can't make a career out of two (in this case *The Ten Commandments* and *The Greatest Show on Earth* (1952)) DeMille pictures, you'd better turn in your suit." This is borne out in the impressive cast of *The Ten Commandments*. Besides Charlton Heston and Vincent Price, there was Edward G Robinson, Yul Brynner, Anne Baxter, John Carradine, Cedric Hardwicke, Yvonne de Carlo and Judith Anderson in the movie.

BELOW Yul Brynner, seen here with Charlton Heston, was named Best Actor of 1956 by the National Board of Review for his performances in *The Ten Commandments, The King and I* and *Anastasia*.

RIGHT According to DeMille, "any 60 pages of the Bible could be turned into a great movie". Anne Baxter in *The Ten Commandments*.

The Ten Commandments relates the story of Moses (played by Heston) who, despite being heir to the Pharaoh (Hardwicke), decides to rejoin the Hebrew slaves from whom his parents came, learning that it is he who has been chosen to take his people to the Promised Land. In his way stands the new Pharaoh, Rameses (Brynner), angered by his bride's continuing love for Moses. Throughout there are plenty of opportunities for the expected epic scenes: the burning bush, the turning of the Nile blood red and, obviously, the parting of the Red Sea. The effects were spectacular enough to win John Fulton an Oscar.

Almost as popular was another Biblical epic starring Charlton Heston, William Wyler's *Ben Hur*, also a remake of a popular silent movie (on which Wyler had worked). It had an equally impressive supporting cast (Jack Hawkins, Sam Jaffe, André Morell, Hugh Griffith) and, at 217 minutes, clocked in only two minutes behind *The Ten Commandments*' mammoth running time. The highlights on this occasion are the breathtaking chariot race and a spectacular sea battle. The sea battle alone ate up $1 million of the $15 million budget and,

with MGM financially shaky during this period, the lavish production was something of a gamble. But it was one that paid off, and even in 1971 *Ben Hur* was still popular enough to attract 32 million Americans to watch a television showing.

The other major fifties money-making epics were another religious extravaganza, *The Robe*, starring Richard Burton, Jean Simmons and Victor Mature and running for a relatively modest 135 minutes; the musical *South Pacific* from Rodgers and Hammerstein, the team behind *The Sound of Music* (1965), which featured Mitzi Gaynor and Rossano Brazzi; and Mike Todd's *Around the World in Eighty Days*, featuring David Niven, Mexican comedian Cantinflas, and 44 stars in cameo roles, which ran at a disappointingly stately pace.

More successful, at least artistically, and more enduring are the four Disney movies in the top 10, with *Peter Pan* just leading *Lady and the Tramp* as the best of the quartet. This is probably due to one of the cinema's great villain's, Captain Hook, and his comic sidekick Smee, as well as the crocodile, sulky fairy Tinkerbell, the Never Land and the vocal talents of young Bobby Driscoll in the title role. However, with "He's a

LEFT "DeMille was firm, but not an authoritarian . . . I found him to be very supportive." Charlton Heston in *The Ten Commandments*.

RIGHT Charlton Heston's second massive Biblical success was for William Wyler in *Ben Hur*. "Willy is beyond question the toughest director I've ever worked for . . . but I'm inclined more and more to the opinion he's also the best," wrote Heston at the time.

RIGHT William Wyler's epic *Ben Hur* was a remake of a popular silent movie on which Wyler had worked.

Tramp", "The Siamese Cat Song" and Peggy Lee, *Lady and the Tramp* definitely has the better music. It also has two winning lead characters and a memorable love scene in an Italian restaurant, as well as the distinction of being the first animated feature produced in CinemaScope.

By comparison, *Sleeping Beauty* is a disappointment, particularly since it took six years and $6,000,000 to produce, making it the most expensive animated feature at the time. Perhaps it would have been better if Walt Disney had been able to devote more time to the movie, but he was busy with other projects, notably Disneyland and his live-action movies. It is one of these live-action movies that completes the Disney quartet, *The Swiss Family Robinson*, a bland and overlong (and therefore typical of these films) adaptation of Johann Wyss' famous novel. It's a pity the Robinsons couldn't have met Captain Hook.

★ NOTABLE FIRST ★

The first actress to appear nude on screen is difficult to identify with any certainty. Among the first and most famous, perhaps because she was later portrayed by Esther Williams in the biopic *Million Dollar Mermaid* (1952), was Australian swimmer and dancer Annette Kellerman. She appeared naked in *Daughter of the Gods* (1916), but was no stranger to controversy, having already popularized the one-piece swimming costume. Pornographic films had actually existed since the early years of the century.

BOX-OFFICE HITS OF THE SIXTIES

		DIRECTOR	DATE	TOTAL RENTALS
1	THE SOUND OF MUSIC	WISE	1965	79,800,000
2	THE JUNGLE BOOK	REITHERMAN	1967	60,964,000
3	LOVE STORY	HILLER	1970	48,700,000
4	DOCTOR ZHIVAGO	LEAN	1965	47,253,762
5	BUTCH CASSIDY AND THE SUNDANCE KID	HILL	1969	46,039,000
6	AIRPORT	SEATON	1970	45,220,118
7	MARY POPPINS	STEVENSON	1964	45,000,000
8	THE GRADUATE	NICHOLS	1967	44,090,729
9	ONE HUNDRED AND ONE DALMATIANS	REITHERMAN/ LUSKE/GERONIMI	1961	38,562,000
10	M*A*S*H	ALTMAN	1970	36,720,000

ABOVE Dean Martin in the *Grand Hotel* of the skies, *Airport*. Its success led to the seventies cycle of disaster movies such as *The Poseidon Adventure* (1972), *Earthquake* (1974) and *The Towering Inferno* (1974).

As far as the box-office is concerned, the sixties offered the greatest diversity: Disney movies, love stories, epics, westerns, disaster melodramas, youth movies, black comedies and, effortlessly top of the heap, an old-fashioned musical.

The success of *The Sound of Music* was probably a foregone conclusion, but the scale must have taken even its makers by surprise. It was based on a long-running Broadway musical; it mixed sentiment, family melodrama, cute kids, religion, romance and popular songs. The songs were the work of the famous Richard Rodgers and Oscar Hammerstein II team;

the director was Robert Wise, an Oscar winner for *West Side Story* (1961), another successful musical with its origins on Broadway; and Julie Andrews was cast in the lead role.

However, at the time, the casting of Andrews as Maria was a risk. She might have been a hit on Broadway, most notably in *My Fair Lady*, but she was rejected in favour of Audrey Hepburn for the film version and hadn't yet had a movie released. In effect, she was an unproven investment as far as cinema was concerned. But director Wise felt otherwise: "Like anybody else we were a little reluctant to go out on a limb and insist on her to the studio for a $7-8 million picture without having seen her on film. So we prevailed on the Disney studios to let us see a couple of sequences of their rough cut (from *Mary Poppins*). The moment we saw her we knew, OHHHHHH!!! This was it. We were crazy about her . . . She was perfect casting, natural, charming, everything."

The film itself can be difficult to criticize objectively. It provokes a strong reaction; people either love all 172 minutes or hate it. It undeniably has a strong opening sequence; the camera gradually coming down the bleak, snow-capped mountain to the greenery of the valley and Julie Andrews bursting into the title song. However, *The Sound of Music* seems interminable, excessively long for such a slight story. In fact, it is almost like a fairy-tale, as gauche young girl becomes governess to seven young children, falls in love with handsome baron and together they ward off the evil Nazis. A

wicked stepmother character is almost introduced in the form of Eleanor Parker, who wants to send the children to boarding school. Even the escape from the Nazis lacks tension.

As a musical, the songs are fairly pedestrian. It lacks the style of Fred Astaire, the energy of Gene Kelly or, looking at its contemporaries, the enthusiasm and memorable songs of *A Hard Day's Night* (1964). The acting cannot save it either: Andrews is frequently overly mannered, Plummer is stiff, the kids insufferably cute and well-meaning, and no one else is given enough to register.

But, to repeat, it is film almost beyond criticism. The millions captivated by it went back time and time again, making *The Sound of Music* the most successful film ever by the end of the sixties. As critic John Gillett wrote, "those allergic to singing nuns and sweetly innocent children" should avoid it.

LEFT Christopher Plummer facing the Nazis in *The Sound of Music;* this still is far more tense than the actual film.

BELOW The children in *The Sound of Music* were considered by many to be too sugary sweet, with no personality.

RIGHT Donald
Sutherland (left) and
Elliott Gould (right) in
Robert Altman's biggest
box-office hit, *M·A·S·H*,
which inspired the
hugely successful
television series.

An infinitely better musical is Disney's superb *The Jungle Book*. But, since it's a Disney cartoon the music is usually overlooked, despite containing such fine songs as "I Wanna Be Like You" and "The Bare Necessities". *The Sound of Music* could have learnt much from this film, not least the economical running time (78 minutes) and a cast of great characters (Baloo the bear, King Louie, Shere Khan and Colonel Hathi). The strength of the characters comes from a faultless combination of excellent animation and perfect voices. Phil Harris as Baloo was so successful that the role was virtually re-created in the next two Disney cartoon features, *The Aristocats* (1970; as Thomas O'Malley the alley cat) and *Robin Hood* (1973; as Little John). And, unlike the almost mechanical Nazis in *The Sound of Music*, there is a real sense of menace from man-eating tiger Shere Khan, voiced by George Sanders. There are, naturally, some complaints, notably the sexist depiction of the girl Mowgli finally falls for, but these are minor. It is a fitting tribute to the talents of Walt Disney, as *The Jungle Book* was the last film he produced. He died on 15 December 1966 from cancer, aged 65.

Not far behind in terms of quality is another Disney cartoon, *One Hundred and One Dalmatians*, which features one of the cinema's great villainesses, Cruella de Vil. The story revolves around Cruella kidnapping the dalmatians to produce a coat from their skins, followed by the dogs' exciting escape. The film marked an important technical advance in animation. It was the first animated feature to use Ub Iwerks' Xerox camera, which could transfer animators' drawings direct to cels. This eliminated the inking process. It also enabled the animators to fill the screen with dalmatians simply by animating a small section and then repeating it.

The third Disney film featured in the sixties top ten was *Mary Poppins*, another over-long Julie Andrews' movie, here making her debut and winning an Oscar. It suffers from an excessive 139 minutes running time, Dick Van Dyke's odd cockney accent and David Tomlinson as a weak male lead. Interestingly, the story bears a marked similarity to *The Sound of Music*, with the strict father, children in need of a loving governess, and the magical Mary Poppins bringing excitement into their lives.

Alongside *The Jungle Book*, the best film to make the top 10 must be Robert Altman's *M∗A∗S∗H*, a black comedy set in the 7077th Mobile Army Surgery Hospital Unit during the Korean War. Typical of Altman, the film concentrates on character and location at the expense of plot, providing Donald Sutherland and Elliott Gould with their best roles. There is his usual over-lapping, improvised dialogue, first-rate supporting characters and a superb set. It was easy to believe people actually lived there. It was very realistic and the public responded well to it. The film's artistic success can be measured by the army's initial ban on screening *M∗A∗S∗H* on its military bases.

The remaining films are the Ryan O'Neal-Ali McGraw *Love Story*, which is now best remembered for its advertising slogan "Love means never having to say you're sorry"; and the David Lean epic *Dr Zhivago*, set during the Russian Revolution, which reunited many of the talents from *Lawrence of Arabia* (1962) – Omar Sharif, scriptwriter Robert Bolt, cinematographer Frederick Young and musician Maurice Jarre. The results were inferior, but brought in more money. Also the all-star melodrama *Airport*, which led to three ludicrous sequels and the entertaining spoof *Airplane* (1980); *The Graduate*, the mildly rebellious Dustin Hoffman youth comedy; and Paul Newman and Robert Redford in the entertaining buddy-buddy western *Butch Cassidy and the Sundance Kid*, featuring the Oscar-winning song "Raindrops Keep Falling on My Head" and a witty script by William Goldman, also the recipient of an Oscar.

BELOW *Butch Cassidy and the Sundance Kid* directly inspired the television series *Alias Smith and Jones* (1971-72) and led to a likeable sequel, *Butch and Sundance: The Early Days* (1979), directed by Richard Lester.

BOX-OFFICE HITS OF THE SEVENTIES

		DIRECTOR	DATE	TOTAL RENTALS
1	STAR WARS	LUCAS	1977	193,500,000
2	THE EMPIRE STRIKES BACK	KERSHNER	1980	141,600,000
3	JAWS	SPIELBERG	1975	129,549,325
4	GREASE	KLEISER	1978	96,300,000
5	THE EXORCIST	FRIEDKIN	1973	89,000,000
6	THE GODFATHER	COPPOLA	1972	86,275,000
7	SUPERMAN	DONNER	1978	82,800,000
8	CLOSE ENCOUNTERS OF THE THIRD KIND	SPIELBERG	1977/80	82,750,000
9	THE STING	HILL	1973	78,212,000
10	SATURDAY NIGHT FEVER	BADHAM	1977	74,100,000

BELOW "I've got a bad feeling about this." Han Solo (Harrison Ford) and Princess Leia (Carrie Fisher) fight it out in *Star Wars*.

Lucas and Spielberg undoubtedly dominated the eighties and they weren't far behind in the seventies, scoring four of the top eight hits (Lucas was the producer of *The Empire Strikes Back*). The outstanding success was *Star Wars*. Unexpectedly it has proved George Lucas's last film as director to date.

Lucas was only 32 when *Star Wars* was released, with just two previous films as director to his credit, a bleak science fiction movie called *THX 1138* (1970) and the wonderful rock'n'roll/nostalgia/coming-of-age movie *American Graffiti* (1973). The latter was a huge success, grossing over $55 million for Universal and earning a place among the decade's top 20 money-earners. Following *American Graffiti*'s release, Lucas turned his attention to an earlier idea, concocted in response to the movies then popular. Lucas felt there was a need for a fantasy movie, saying: "Young people today don't have a fantasy life; not the way we did. All the films they see are movies of disaster and realistic violence."

So he looked to the comic strips and serials he'd enjoyed as a youngster. "Originally, I wanted to make a *Flash Gordon* movie, with all the trimmings, but I couldn't obtain the rights to the characters. So I began researching and went right back and found where Alex Raymond [*Flash Gordon*'s creator] had got his idea from." And so work commenced. "I began writing *Star Wars* in January 1973 – eight hours a day, five days a week – from then until March 1976 when we began shooting. Even then I was busy doing rewrites in the evenings after the day's work. In fact, I wrote four entirely different screenplays for *Star Wars*, searching for just the right ingredients, characters and story line."

All this effort paid off – handsomely. *Star Wars* was a box-office sensation, as well as a fair critical success. And it is a good movie. It very obviously draws on past films and traditions, wrapping them up with some breathtaking special effects to produce an energetic, enthusiastic and exciting whole. The most obvious reference of *Star Wars* is to westerns; the killing of Luke Skywalker's family is a direct steal from John Ford's *The Searchers* (1956) and Harrison Ford's Han Solo is given a black waistcoat and gun belt, thus resembling a gunslinger. But the references also enhance the movie. For example, *The Searchers* episode establishes Luke, like the John Wayne character in the Ford film, as an outsider, a position that is firmly underlined in the final *Star Wars* movie, *Return of the Jedi* (1983).

Further references are plentiful: the Second World War movie – particularly *The Dam Busters* (1954) during the final raid on the Death Star; swashbucklers – with would-be Jedi knight Luke Skywalker and Princess Leia swinging on a rope in the vast spaceship; old serials – the written opening chapter introduction relating the story so far; *Flash Gordon* – the Sand People are reminiscent of the old Buster Crabbe serials; fairytales – evil Darth Vader kidnapping the beautiful Princess; and Laurel and Hardy – robot comedy team C3PO and R2D2. Lucas even draws from Nazi propaganda movies, specifically Leni Riefenstahl's *Triumph of the Will* (1936) for the final medal ceremony.

More importantly, Lucas also got the basics right. He balanced a trio of fresh-faced, enthusiastic and relatively unknown performers (Mark Hamill, Harrison Ford, Carrie Fisher) with some first-rate, experienced actors (Alec Guinness, Peter Cushing). Furthermore, the characters were

ABOVE George Lucas' *Star Wars*, in 1977 Hollywood's most commercially successful movie.

RIGHT A classic quartet: Mark Hammill, Harrison Ford, Chewbacca and Carrie Fisher in *Star Wars*.

BELOW R2D2 and C3PO in *Star Wars* regrettably led to a flood of insufferably cute robots in science-fiction movies during the seventies.

well drawn. As Harrison Ford perceptibly observed: "I think that it was not the hardware that made *Star Wars* a success, but its unique vision . . . People would have no emotional attachment to that environment without human characters to be attracted to. Otherwise, it's just 'Oh, wow, oh, wow'. Lucas's genius was that he gave those robots a totally human character."

Nevertheless, hardware undoubtedly helped. The audience is impressed from the start, when a huge spaceship takes an eternity to fly across the screen (a scene which became a science fiction cliché, to the extent that it was spoofed in Mel Brooks' *Spaceballs* (1987)). Such was their success, they never seem like effects, simply part of the story.

The success of *Star Wars* demanded sequels. Fortunately, for once, this had always been the intention; for example, Jabba the Hut, later featured in *Return of the Jedi*, is mentioned in passing during *Star Wars*. *Star Wars* was merely chapter four in a nine-part story, with chapters five and six given over to the same characters. The next instalment arrived three years later. *The Empire Strikes Back*, amazingly, was not a

disappointment. It was the second-biggest hit of the decade and thoughtfully developed the universe created in *Star Wars*. It was a richer, more complex film, although it lacked the original's overwhelming enthusiasm, and in Yoda introduced another fascinating character. It is probably the strongest film of the trilogy.

Both are certainly better than the other two science fiction movies in the seventies top 10, *Superman* and *Close Encounters of the Third Kind*. *Superman* in particular was a disappointment, especially given its $40 million budget as opposed to *Star Wars*' (relatively) paltry $10.5 million. The omens were bad from the start for *Superman*, as the film's 30-week shooting schedule stretched to 65, naturally requiring an extensive revision of the original $25 million budget. Perhaps warning bells should have rung earlier when producer Alexander Salkind first suggested the project to his co-producer father Ilya and he admitted that he had never even heard of *Superman*. This didn't augur well for the future.

This possibly accounts for some of the film's problems. Where *Star Wars* quickly and economically established characters and situations, *Superman* wasted much of its running time on dull exposition. This is all the more regrettable since

LEFT The popular Yoda, Luke Skywalker's teacher in the ways of The Force, in *The Empire Strikes Back*.

LEFT Chewbacca and Princess Leia in *The Empire Strikes Back*, whose enormous $22 million budget was more than double that for *Star Wars*.

Reeve they found the perfect Superman, although he alone could not save the movie. Nevertheless, financially the film was successful enough to produce three sequels, starting relatively promisingly with Richard Lester's *Superman II* (1980) but rapidly descending to the painfully tatty *Superman IV: The Quest for Peace* (1987).

Steven Spielberg's *Close Encounters of the Third Kind* is a better movie, although hardly deserving the widespread praise it received on its initial release, which often focused on the film's supposed sense of wonder and its benign aliens. The most interesting section deals with Richard Dreyfuss' obsession with the UFO he spotted and the effect this has on his family. When Spielberg came to prepare *Close Encounters of the Third Kind: The Special Edition* in 1980, this was the section he trimmed. It is difficult to disagree with film critic Derek Malcolm when he wrote, "One is inclined to feel that with all the money at his disposal, Spielberg might have got it right the first time". John Williams provided the music for all four of the science fiction hits.

Williams also provided the music, and won an Oscar for, the other Spielberg movie in the top ten, *Jaws*, a far superior film to *Close Encounters*. Much of its power comes from the simplicity of the story, coupled with a strong cast (Richard Dreyfuss, Robert Shaw, Roy Scheider). The story is set in a small tourist resort which is plagued by shark attacks, with the sheriff (Scheider) in conflict with the mayor (Murray Hamilton) over the best course of action. The climax is Scheider, Shaw and Dreyfuss tracking down the killer shark.

ABOVE "If someone had told me in advance that the film was going to take nearly two years out of my life, that I was going to have to come to England, change my physique, change my entire lifestyle, I probably wouldn't have done it." Christopher Reeve as Superman.

RIGHT The Mother ship hovers over Devil's Tower before landing in Spielberg's *Close Encounters of the Third Kind.*

the most enjoyable performance comes from Gene Hackman as the evil Lex Luther, who is given little screen time early on. In a better film Hackman would have been annoyingly over-the-top; in *Superman* he enlivens a dull movie, certainly more so than Marlon Brando. The casting of Brando provided most of the pre-release publicity, mainly centring on his $3 million fee for 12 days' filming.

More problematic was the casting of the Clark Kent/Superman role. Initially the Salkinds had felt that, to raise the large budget, they needed a star name in the title role. Thus Robert Redford, Burt Reynolds, James Caan *et al* were all, somewhat improbably, linked with the part. Thankfully the supporting cast was considered a sufficient draw and the Salkinds were free to cast an unknown. And in Christopher

ABOVE *Close Encounters of the Third Kind* took Spielberg two attempts to get right. He released *Close Encounters of the Third Kind: The Special Edition* in 1980.

LEFT Cary Guffey in the highly successful *Close Encounters of the Third Kind.*

Jaws is the best revenge-of-nature movie since Hitchcock's *The Birds* (1963), so not surprisingly spawned four poor sequels and a host of even worse imitations, the Joe Dante-directed, Roger Corman-produced *Piranha* (1978) being a notable exception. *Jaws* in turn bears a remarkable similarity to one of Spielberg's earlier films, the even better *Duel* (1971), in which an unidentified driver of a large truck (which becomes the shark in *Jaws*) motivelessly terrorizes Dennis Weaver (instead of the town).

The Exorcist was marketed as the scariest film ever. It isn't. In fact *Jaws*, which was aimed at the family audience, is more gripping. But the publicity was hugely effective and there were some sensational scenes for the media to exploit: the 12-year-old Regan (Linda Blair) vomiting green bile, uttering a stream of obscenities (at a priest, no less), her head rotating 360 degrees, and performing sexual acts with a crucifix. In fact, the author and producer William Peter Blatty felt director William Friedkin went too far in this scene.

There are good things in *The Exorcist* – the opening sequence in Iraq, Max Von Sydow and Lee J Cobb, the world

ABOVE Big budget horror: Max Von Sydow and Jason Miller in *The Exorcist*. Surprisingly, it was considered respectable enough to be nominated for the Best Picture Oscar and won 1973's Golden Globe as Best Drama.

RIGHT Richard Dreyfuss and Roy Scheider in *Jaws*, one of Spielberg's better successes, based on Peter Benchley's best-selling novel.

LEFT Olivia Newton-John and John Travolta in Ronald Keiser's fifties set musical *Grease*. It is difficult to imagine Gene Vincent, Buddy Holly or Eddie Cochran approving.

BELOW "We'll make him an offer he can't refuse." Marlon Brando in Francis Ford Coppola's *The Godfather*.

in decay subtext – but ultimately it's a huge disappointment. Central to the disappointment is the film's poor pacing. Equally damaging is the lack of concern created for either the mother (Ellen Burstyn) or the possessed Regan; both noticeably reduce the chills. However, like *Jaws*, it was responsible for a flood of mainly worthless imitations.

Of the remaining films, two were musicals from John Travolta's 15 minutes at the top of the box-office heap. The fifties nostalgia of *Grease* is more likeable than the seventies disco of *Saturday Night Fever*, but is still not a patch on *American Graffiti*. Both led to terrible sequels, *Grease 2* (1982) and the Sylvester Stallone-directed *Staying Alive* (1983).

Undoubtedly the critics' favourite among the top ten would be Francis Ford Coppola's epic, 175-minute Mafia movie *The Godfather*. It's a fine film with an outstanding cast (Brando, Caan, Pacino, Duvall, Keaton, Conte). *The Godfather*, unusually, deserved the Best Picture Oscar it won and, even more unusually, led to an even better sequel, *The Godfather Part 2* (1974), which also received the Best Picture Oscar. Unfortunately, *Part 3* (1990) was a disappointment and was rightfully overshadowed by Martin Scorsese's gangster movie *Goodfellas* (1990), released at the same time.

BOX-OFFICE HITS OF THE EIGHTIES

		DIRECTOR	DATE	TOTAL RENTALS
1	ET THE EXTRA-TERRESTRIAL	SPIELBERG	1982	
2	RETURN OF THE JEDI	MARQUAND	1983	228,618,939
3	BATMAN	BURTON	1989	168,002,414
4	GHOSTBUSTERS	REITMAN	1984	150,500,000
5	RAIDERS OF THE LOST ARK	SPIELBERG	1981	132,720,000
6	INDIANA JONES AND THE LAST CRUSADE	SPIELBERG	1989	115,598,000
7	INDIANA JONES AND THE TEMPLE OF DOOM	SPIELBERG	1984	115,500,000
8	BEVERLY HILLS COP	BREST	1984	109,000,000
9	BACK TO THE FUTURE	ZEMECKIS	1985	108,000,000
10	TOOTSIE	POLLACK	1982	105,493,534
				94,910,000

The fantasy/adventure genre dominated the box-office throughout the eighties, chiefly through the vision of two men: George Lucas, who produced *Return of the Jedi* and the *Indiana Jones* trilogy, and Steven Spielberg, director of four of the top-10 hits and executive producer of *Back to the Future*. Theirs is a rather backward-looking vision, returning both to the small-town America of the fifties (made explicit in *Back to the Future*) and the simplistic morality and direct action of thirties' serials. Regrettably, the darkest film Spielberg lent his name to during this period, Joe Dante's *Gremlins* (1984), failed to penetrate the top 10 and was financially eclipsed by the banal *Ghostbusters*. Nevertheless, the film returned a very healthy $79,500,000.

Towering above all of Spielberg's other achievements, at least financially, is *ET The Extra-Terrestrial*, often referred to as his most personal movie (note Dee Wallace reading *Peter Pan*, a long-cherished project of Spielberg's). Surprisingly, the director now claims to have had doubts initially about the film's appeal. "Believe it or not, I never thought *ET* would be a big commercial success. I thought it was my first personal movie, and I did not know it would be as infectious as it turned out to be." His most personal movie it may be, but it was one with a highly effective publicity department and merchanidising machine. They were successful enough to ensure that by the time the film opened in Britain, many people had already seen Spielberg's movie on often poor quality, much sought-after, pirate videos.

Spielberg quickly establishes his preferred milieu: small-town, exclusively white, America. This is a place where Mr

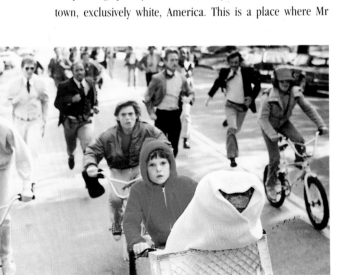

Smith, Mr Deeds and an assortment of Frank Capra heroes might have grown up; it is safe for kids to be out alone at night; no one appears to be poor; and friends and family can always be relied on to rally round. It is just as if the sixties never happened; it might not be the world we know, but the appeal is obviously strong. To this Spielberg sensibly adds a contemporary gloss, including BMX bikes, Dungeons and Dragons and Elvis Costello on the soundtrack.

Spielberg immediately directs audience sympathy completely towards ET from the opening sequence showing ET's spaceship accidentally leaving him behind on Earth; no doubts are ever permitted. ET is cute, lovable and harmless. At first, ET is seen in long shot dwarfed by huge trees, immediately

ABOVE Spielberg directs audience sympathy towards ET by portraying ET as cute, lovable and harmless. In this still ET has been dressed up by the children for Halloween.

LEFT The final escape bid in *ET* was particularly exciting, with ET hidden in a sheet and Henry Thomas pushing ET along.

RIGHT Henry Thomas with Carlo Rimbaldi's world-famous creation, ET. *ET* is considered Spielberg's most personal movie.

BELOW Steven Spielberg with Henry Thomas, who gave an excellent performance in *ET*.

followed by a point-of-view shot of the same trees endlessly stretching towards the sky. How could such a creature be threatening? By contrast, the humans appear menacing. From the first their car gratingly intrudes on John Williams' sugary score; their faces are not shown. They are seen either in silhouette or through close-ups of their jangling keys. All this is seen from ET's point of view, his height approximating that of a small child. In fact, much of the film is shot as if the action were being observed by a child. This careful manipulation of our emotions is supremely maintained throughout by Spielberg.

The story is of ET's friendship with a young boy named EllioT, and Elliott's increasing awareness that ET must return home to survive. It's also about Elliott's growing up. Early in the film his brother, Michael, tells him: "Why don't you grow

LEFT Jack Nicholson's over-the-top performance as The Joker in Tim Burton's *Batman* reportedly earned him $50 million.

up? Think about somebody else's feelings." He not only thinks about ET's feelings, he literally *feels* them.

Much has also been made of the parallel between ET and Christ: both have healing powers and both are resurrected. However, the latter is an archetypal device (it's known as "having your cake and eating it") and could equally be Spielberg drawing on his love of Disney. For example, Balloo is wrongly thought to have died in *The Jungle Book* (1967), as is Trusty in *Lady and the Tramp* (1955). In fact, *Variety* called *ET* "the best Disney film Disney never made". There is also more than an element of *The Wizard of Oz* (1939) philosophy in *ET*. After all, there is no place like home.

The film is technically impeccable. It incorporates Carlo Rimbaldi's design of ET, John Williams' Oscar-winning music, Industrial Light and Magic's special effects and Allen Daviau's

excellent cinematography. The acting is equally well-judged, particularly from Henry Thomas as Elliott, who thankfully avoids the dual evils of cloying and cute. Even Harvey the dog turns in a fine performance. The film is by turns moving, funny – ET avoiding discovery by pretending to be a stuffed toy – and exciting, particularly the final escape bid. But it is not flawless. Some of the comedy is particularly ill-judged – for example, the send-up of *The Quiet Man* (1952) – and the arrival of the government agents and scientists is overly melodramatic. And it's a pity Spielberg directs our emotions so calculatingly, thus allowing absolutely no room for doubts.

It is a far better film than most other movies on the top 10 (*Jedi* and *Raiders* excepted), particularly *Batman* and *Ghostbusters*. *Batman* has little to recommend it outside its stunning set design. Michael Keaton is a disappointingly weak

RIGHT Michael Keaton
proved a
disappointingly weak
Batman. The movie was
highly overrated.

BELOW Actors Dan
Akroyd and Harold
Ramis also wrote the
script for *Ghostbusters*.

Bruce Wayne, making 'The Batman' appear to be more wish-fulfilment on Wayne's part than another side of the same person. The notion that 'The Joker' is his *alter ego* (he was created by "The Batman" when pushed into a vat of toxic waste) is also undermined by this weakness. But then Jack Nicholson's ridiculously over-the-top performance had already robbed 'The Joker' of the menace all great villains should possess. There is even less to recommend in Dan Aykroyd's pet project *Ghostbusters*, aside from the presence of Rick Moranis and Bill Murray. Its success can perhaps be attributed chiefly to Ray Parker Jnr's catchy hit theme song.

Far more successful was the first Lucas-Spielberg collaboration. *Raiders of the Lost Ark*, which introduced Harrison Ford's whip-carrying Indiana Jones. Thankfully, the initial choice, Tom Selleck, was unavailable. The film was obviously inspired

LEFT "It was a very collaborative atmosphere, and that's the way I like to work." Harrison Ford in the first and best Indiana Jones movies, *Raiders of the Lost Ark*.

by the old Saturday morning serials, and Spielberg reportedly screened the likes of *Ace Drummond* (1936) and *Fighting Devil Dogs* (1938) before filming. The result was the best action-adventure movie of the decade, effortlessly eclipsing the tired James Bond series or indeed its own two sequels. It is also superior to its original inspirations, *Flash Gordon* (1936) and Larry Buster Crabbe aside, of course. But then, given its $22 million budget, it really should be.

Set in 1936, the film revolves around the search for the Ark of the Covenant, which held Moses's Ten Commandments and is believed to have incredible powers. In the wrong hands such powers could be devastatingly destructive, and the Nazis, the ultimate hissable Hollywood villains, are definitely the wrong hands. In common with the other Spielberg movies, *Raiders of the Lost Ark* is a film that demands to be seen at the cinema. As the director comments: "It's a group experience for large numbers of people sitting in movie theatres, not for two or three people sitting in front of the television at home. You need to feel the audience clapping and laughing and yelling and screaming in order to get the total effect of the Indiana Jones saga."

Such was *Raiders*' success that Universal opened the sequel one minute past midnight on its first day of release. *Temple of Doom* was so eagerly awaited that people queued for 18 hours for these first screenings. Unfortunately, it is nowhere near the equal of its predecessor. Not the least of its troubles is the heroine. Where Karen Allen had been a feisty and likeable partner, Kate Capshaw was simply a wimp, almost the archetypal dizzy blonde. And perhaps the tongues were slightly too far in cheek this time. After all, the leading characters were all named after dogs, which is surely tempting fate. Indiana belonged to Lucas, Spielberg's dog is called Willie (Capshaw's character) and Short Round (the increasingly obligatory annoying brat found in such films) was one of the

BELOW Paramount's $14 million investment in the Eddie Murphy comedy *Beverly Hills Cop* brought in $108 million at the North American box-office.

scriptwriters' dogs. There are still highlights, of course, most notably the breathtaking roller-coaster ride through the mines near the film's climax.

Next time out Spielberg and Lucas cast Sean Connery in the role of Ford's partner, this time his father, despite there being only 12 years difference in the actors' ages. It probably sealed the film's financial success, if it was ever in doubt, but *The Last Crusade* still failed to live up to the original.

The exceptions to the domination of the fantasy genre have been two comedies: a routine starring-vehicle, *Beverly Hills Cop*, for Eddie Murphy and the self-important *Tootsie*. *Tootsie* has grand pretensions to deal with sexism, although dressing Dustin Hoffman in drag to examine the subject seems perilously close to sexist. How about casting a woman in the leading role in a film about sexism? As good as many of these films undoubtedly are, it is regrettable that the top money-makers do not exhibit a little more variety.

★ NOTABLE FIRST ★

Hollywood's first 3-D feature film was a routine programme called *Bwana Devil* (1952), written, produced and directed by Arch Oboler, who was famed for his work in radio. This African adventure movie starred Robert Stack, Barbara Britton and Nigel Bruce and inspired over 30 generally routine imitations during the next couple of years, the best being *House of Wax* (1953). In fact, *Bwana Devil* was not the first 3-D picture. The process already had a long history, a number of shorts having appeared in the twenties and Italy producing the first 3-D feature, *Nozze Vagabond*, in 1936. Despite being panned by the critics, *Bwana Devil* was a big success.

ABOVE Dustin Hoffman, seen here with director Sydney Pollack, earned an Oscar nomination for his performance as struggling actor Michael Dorsey who turns into successful soap star Beverly Michaels in *Tootsie*.

THE MOST EXPENSIVE FILM

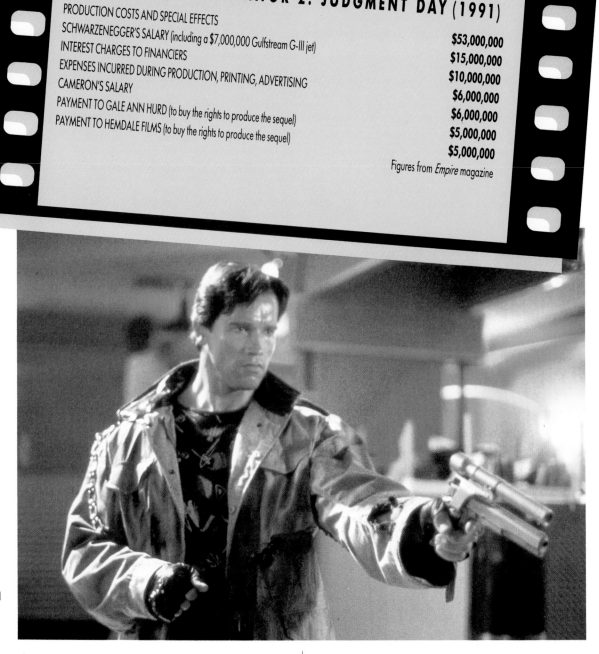

BUDGET OF TERMINATOR 2: JUDGMENT DAY (1991)

PRODUCTION COSTS AND SPECIAL EFFECTS	$53,000,000
SCHWARZENEGGER'S SALARY (including a $7,000,000 Gulfstream G-III jet)	$15,000,000
INTEREST CHARGES TO FINANCIERS	$10,000,000
EXPENSES INCURRED DURING PRODUCTION, PRINTING, ADVERTISING	$6,000,000
CAMERON'S SALARY	$6,000,000
PAYMENT TO GALE ANN HURD (to buy the rights to produce the sequel)	$5,000,000
PAYMENT TO HEMDALE FILMS (to buy the rights to produce the sequel)	$5,000,000

Figures from *Empire* magazine

RIGHT "I didn't write the first film with a preconceived notion of doing a sequel," said James Cameron. Arnold Schwarzenegger in *The Terminator*.

LEFT Arnold
Schwarzenegger,
Edward Furlong and
Linda Hamilton in
Terminator 2.

Arnold Schwarzenegger may have spoken only 74 words during *The Terminator* (1984), but three proved particularly ominous: "I'll be back." Seven years later he was, with a vengeance, in "the world's most expensive movie", James Cameron's *Terminator 2: Judgment Day* (1991). As far as production company Carolco is concerned, it seems to be a slightly unwanted tag and the exact budget remains a mystery, variously reported at between $88 and $115 million. $100 million is probably fairly near the mark. However, given constantly escalating production costs and the resounding success of *Terminator 2*, it may be a title quickly relinquished.

In comparison, the original *Terminator* had a slender $6 million budget, was directed by Cameron when his only previous directorial credit was *Piranha II: Flying Killers* (1981) and was released to lukewarm reviews. Nevertheless, it became one of the decade's major cult movies and earned a healthy profit for Hemdale Films. A sequel seemed assured,

but neither Schwarzenegger nor Cameron was keen to work for Hemdale a second time, feeling they would again be hampered by insufficient budget. So in stepped Carolco, which also produced the Schwarzenegger-Verhoeven sci-fi movie *Total Recall* (1990), with the money to buy out Hemdale Films and Gale Ann Hurd, the original co-producer with Cameron and his ex-wife. Carolco's only condition was that Cameron must meet a 4 July 1991 release date, a mere 18 months away. After completion, Cameron said: "It was not only a logistically difficult picture, a technically difficult picture and a dramatically ambitious picture, it also had to be done on a ridiculously short schedule."

When the script was first shown to art director Joe Nemec his "first response . . . was exhaustion. There was just so much there; and since Jim is a perfectionist, I knew he would want it all done absolutely first-rate." It's lucky he didn't see an earlier draft which, according to co-writer William Wisher,

RIGHT The new Arnold Schwarzenegger turns hero in *Terminator 2: Judgment Day*, the most expensive movie ever made.

would have required a $200 million budget. After ditching the idea of Schwarzenegger playing two Terminators, one good and one bad, Cameron and Wisher soon settled on the final story. It needed to take into account Schwarzenegger's new, softer, post-*Kindergarten Cop* (1990) image, which meant transferring much of the aggression to Linda Hamilton's character. According to Cameron: "Arnold's role globally has changed and he is a great idol to children and people everywhere. I think it's very fortunate for me that the story that I came up with many years ago involved a change of the character of the Terminator to where he is now essentially the hero of the film."

Set 10 years after the original, a more advanced T-1000 Terminator (Robert Patrick) is sent back from the 21st century to kill John Connor, a young boy (played by newcomer Edward Furlong) destined to become the leader of the human resistance in the future war between man and machines. The adult John Connor, therefore, sends a T-800 Terminator (Arnold Schwarzenegger, naturally), seen in the original movie, to protect his childhood self. The T-1000 takes the form of a patrol cop while the T-800 resembles a biker, dressed in black from head to toe. Meanwhile, John's mother, Sarah Connor (Linda Hamilton, also repeating her role from the original movie), is held in a state hospital, considered crazy after her experiences with the original Terminator.

The story naturally progresses into a series of superb action set pieces, maintaining a staggering pace throughout its 135-minute running time. For once, the massive budget is strongly in evidence on screen, with some awesome stunts and special effects. Most importantly, Schwarzenegger is believably established as the underdog, no mean achievement, particularly given Patrick's obvious physical inferiority. Cameron aimed to create "something that was more terrifying than the Terminator, and yet didn't look any more overtly inhuman". This was partly done by making the T-1000 a shape-shifter, using similar effects to those found in John Carpenter's *The Thing* (1982) and Cameron's own *The Abyss* (1989). The results are stunning.

However, Patrick must also take much of the credit for a good performance, registering strongly with little dialogue, projecting a steely menace with his eyes. "One of the things I did with my eyes was to hold them on the target, never blinking. I would lock onto a target, as if there was a straight

LEFT "When I was a kid I had a lot of dreams about nuclear wars," said James Cameron. Schwarzenegger and Edward Furlong at *Terminor 2*'s climax.

line between us, and then my body would just carry me there, smoothly and without effort." He almost steals the film from Arnold Schwarzenegger.

The other unknown, child actor Edward Furlong, unfortunately is not a success. He functions as the now obligatory, wisecracking, annoying brat, presumably as an identifiable character for young teenagers. The film also suffers from a certain amount of pretentiousness, Cameron calling it "the first action movie to advocate world peace". It also features some corny statements – "If a machine can learn the value of human life, then maybe we can too" – during Sarah Connor's voice-over, and in John Connor features a second JC who will save the world.

At the time of release Schwarzeneggar was the most bankable star in America, Germany and Japan, and only marginally behind Mel Gibson in Britain. From the first day, when it grossed $12 million, *Terminator 2* was a huge success. Within two days its takings had outstripped that of the original *Terminator*, the production costs were recovered in 12 days and by the end of its third week *Terminator 2* had taken $115 million. The massive investment had obviously paid off, commercially and critically, most critics being happy to echo Cameron's partner Larry Kasanoff's belief that *Terminator 2* will give audiences "the best roller-coaster ride of their lives, they'll be thrilled". But for $100 million, they should be.

THE BIGGEST FLOP

ABOVE "The film is a masterpiece," wrote critic Nigel Andrews as *Heaven's Gate* was reassessed following the British release of the full version. Kris Kristofferson and Michael Cimino seen on location of the film.

RIGHT "You never answer anything personal," – Isabelle Huppert to Kris Kristofferson in *Heaven's Gate*.

To state categorically which film is the biggest flop is impossible. What criterion should be used? Should it be the difference between budget and box-office takings or the ratio of budget to earnings? Neither is quite satisfactory. Even if this could be agreed upon, film companies are obviously reticent about making public the details of their failures. However, there can be no doubt about which box-office failure has attracted the most publicity over the past 25 years: Michael Cimino's *Heaven's Gate* (1980). Its budget rapidly spiralled from $7.5 million to somewhere in the $36-40 million bracket. And, in return for their investment, United Artists received just $1.5 million back at the American box-office, resulting in their company being taken over by MGM.

So, why did *Heaven's Gate*'s budget and shooting schedule increase so dramatically? According to Cimino, interviewed at the time of the film's release, "part of the cost was in creating departments for the purpose of making one movie, that used to exist for the making of many movies. We literally had to create a studio for the making of this one film." While this is, at best, rather dubious, problems were caused by Cimino's meticulous, some might say obsessive, attention to detail.

"The difficulties were in the sheer amount of time and work, close to six months finding locations and another six months of research – very extensive – conducted all over the United States. For example, we drove 20,000 miles in the State of Colorado looking for places that were new and exciting visually." This naturally created problems. The town of Sweetwater was constructed in the Glacier National Park and was "built on platforms three feet above the ground, so as not to spoil the National Park grass beneath it". Similarly, Cimino's assistants scoured America for the correct train to be used for Kristofferson's arrival at Caspar. One was finally located in Denver and transported across five states.

But why wasn't producer Joann Carelli able to control Cimino's extravagance? More to the point, why did United Artists allow Cimino such control? The answer to the second question lies in the success of Cimino's previous film, the Oscar-winning and lengthy *The Deer Hunter* (1978), which was listed at number 10 in *Variety*'s 1979 box-office hits with takings of $26,927,000. Meanwhile, Carelli claims "things probably never would have gotten to the point they did if there had been proper support for the film's producer from the studio. Countless times, I would be arguing out a problem

ABOVE Another spectacular crowd scene set in Caspar City, from *Heaven's Gate*.

with Michael and would call to get the company that's paying for the picture to back me up. Usually they'd tell me they couldn't talk . . . they were too busy." In a classic example of being wise after the event, United Artists' president Norbert Auerbach said: "In my opinion creative freedom was carried a bit too far."

So, why did such an expensive film fail? Cimino places much of the blame on the venom with which the critics greeted the film (*New York Times*' Vincent Canby considered it an unmitigated disaster, while Andrew Sarris wrote of "the stupidity and incoherence of *Heaven's Gate*" in *Village Voice*). Cimino defended the movie, saying of his critics, "They cannot tolerate the truth of their original fratricide during the conquest of the old west." They also panned the film tech-

nically, despite Zsigmon's superb cinematography which was also denigrated. Nevertheless, the film made $39,000 in its first, and only, week at New York's cinema 1 in November 1980. However, United Artists panicked and the day after its release announced *Heaven's Gate* was being pulled in New York and Toronto, and would not be opening in Los Angeles. Instead, Cimino was to re-edit, cutting the 219 minutes down to 130 minutes, which would allow more screenings per day. The critics were no kinder to the film when it reopened in April 1981, and if United Artists hoped for a better response from European critics and audiences, they were to be disappointed. When shown at Cannes, French director and jury president Jacques Deray could only say, "we found a lack of understanding of the story and of the characters".

ABOVE "I don't believe in words and dialogue. They're quickly useless. One can only get near to people when taking time to watch them live," claimed Cimino. Caspar City in *Heaven's Gate*.

The largest film set was built for Anthony Mann's *The Fall of the Roman Empire* (1964). The forum set measured 1312ft by 754ft (400m by 230m) and the film finally cost $20,000,000. Despite the presence of stars like Alec Guinness, Sophia Loren, James Mason and Stephen Boyd, the film only grossed £1,900,000 on its initial American release.

So, what of the film? *Heaven's Gate* is an outstanding film, and one with a growing reputation, particularly in Europe after the original version was released. Dilys Powell thought it "magnificent" and David Castell considered it "the major western (of its period)". Watching the film 10 years later, it becomes increasingly difficult to understand the hatred *Heaven's Gate* originally generated. It is equally difficult to comprehend how United Artists could believe that such a complex and pessimistic western would recoup a $40 million budget. The dialogue is critical of the ruling class ("You are all evil here. You call this a free country?"; "It's getting dangerous to be poor in this country."); the ending, where Huppert is murdered and Kristofferson shown old and dis-

illusioned, is downbeat; and one of the central themes is the sense of loss and ageing. Hardly a combination that would endear itself to the American public; nor, it seems, to the critics. The debate will go on it seems.

The film opens at Harvard in 1872, where Kris Kristofferson and John Hurt are graduating. Twenty years later, they are on opposite sides in the Johnson County War, in which a group of Wyoming cattle barons, called the Stockgrowers' Association, attempts to wipe out mostly immigrant homesteaders with the tacit approval of the Federal authorities. To do so they create a death list of 125 names. Kristofferson plays the lawman who stands with the ranchers against the powerful cattlemen, who are led by Sam Waterston and aided by hired gun Christopher Walken as their foreman. In between is Isabelle Huppert, the madam of the local brothel, with whom both Kristofferson and Walken are in love.

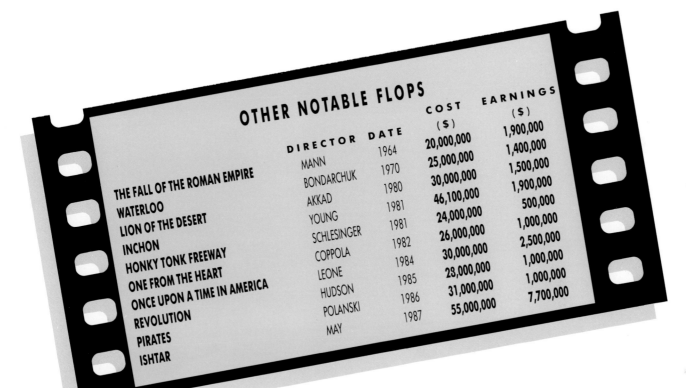

OTHER NOTABLE FLOPS

	DIRECTOR	DATE	COST ($)	EARNINGS ($)
THE FALL OF THE ROMAN EMPIRE	MANN	1964	20,000,000	1,900,000
WATERLOO	BONDARCHUK	1970	25,000,000	1,400,000
LION OF THE DESERT	AKKAD	1980	30,000,000	1,500,000
INCHON	YOUNG	1981	46,100,000	1,900,000
HONKY TONK FREEWAY	SCHLESINGER	1981	24,000,000	500,000
ONE FROM THE HEART	COPPOLA	1982	26,000,000	1,000,000
ONCE UPON A TIME IN AMERICA	LEONE	1984	30,000,000	2,500,000
REVOLUTION	HUDSON	1985	28,000,000	1,000,000
PIRATES	POLANSKI	1986	31,000,000	1,000,000
ISHTAR	MAY	1987	55,000,000	7,700,000

Technically *Heaven's Gate* is excellent, with its huge budget well in evidence. David Mansfield's wonderful music is particularly effective in the lyrical roller-skating sequence, a wonderful celebration of community that ensures we care for these settlers; Vilmos Zsigmond's at-times sepia-like photography is outstanding; the sets and period detail seem impeccable; and the use of thousands of extras works dramatically. The large crowd scenes, the overflowing city, are important in establishing the realism of the piece, besides creating a sensation of both a country on the move and a period of change. These scenes are thus concentrated into the first hour. After that they are no longer necessary, having served their function. The main technical complaint is the sound, with dialogue frequently difficult to comprehend – there can never have been a noisier city than Caspar. Nevertheless, this further enhances the realism; we do believe Caspar is a real city. All these elements combine to create an overwhelming whole, producing a film that refreshingly was made to be seen on a big screen.

Heaven's Gate is obviously not flawless: the opening Harvard prologue would improve if it were cut from 20 to 10 minutes,

Jeff Bridges' character is underdeveloped, and John Hurt seems to belong to another movie. But it is an intelligent film of frequently breathtaking grandeur. Instead of being remembered as the cinema's most notorious failure, *Heaven's Gate* should be considered alongside *McCabe and Mrs Miller* (1971), with which it bears some comparison, as one of the top five westerns of the past 20 years.

ABOVE Warren Beatty and Dustin Hoffman's great box-office flop, *Ishtar*, not a patch on *Road to Morocco* (1942).

The Stars

TOP BOX-OFFICE MALE STARS

BOTTOM RIGHT Will Rogers with Farrell's regular partner Janet Gaynor in *State Fair* (1933).

BELOW Charles Farrell with Janet Gaynor in Frank Borzage's classic silent weepie *Seventh Heaven*, remade 10 years later with James Stewart.

uigley Publications hold an annual poll among film exhibitors, asking them to name the most popular stars that year. The Quigley poll is only an approximate guide, for example favouring the more prolific stars; Dean Martin and Jerry Lewis were the top stars of 1952, but had made five films between 1951 and 1952. Perhaps this explains the absence of Cary Grant and Humphrey Bogart, Steve McQueen and Mel Gibson. Nevertheless, Quigley provides a reasonable indication of public taste, and remains the source most frequently quoted.

The first half of the thirties was dominated by Fox stars (Charles Farrell and Will Rogers), while the second belonged to MGM (Clark Gable and Mickey Rooney). However, MGM also scored an early success in 1930 with William Haines, its first star to appear in a talkie with *Alias Jimmy Valentine*

(1928). He went on to appear in routine movies like *Speedway* (1929) and *The Duke Steps Out* (1929).

The almost-forgotten Farrell made his best film in the silent era, the classic weepie *Seventh Heaven* (1927), with his frequent partner Janet Gaynor, the biggest female star of 1931 and 1934. They appeared together on 12 occasions and during the early thirties starred in the musicals *Sunny Side Up* (1929) and *High Society Blues* (1930), the fantasy *Liliom* (1930) and the drama *Tess of the Storm Country* (1932). By 1933 Farrell no longer featured in the Quigley poll, but had further success on television, particularly in the popular *My Little Margie* (1952-54). In the comedian Will Rogers, Fox had another hugely successful star, his reign ending only with his death, aged 54, in an airplane crash on 15 August 1935. Rogers had been in films since 1918, but his golden era was the thirties. He starred in the early sound version of Mark

LEFT "He (Clark Gable) possesses a grand sense of humour, and has a most attractive speaking voice" – Florence Desmond for Careeras' cigarette cards.

Twain's *A Connecticut Yankee* (1931) and had a huge hit with the family drama *State Fair* (1933), which also featured Janet Gaynor. These were followed by the equally popular *Judge Priest* (1934) directed by John Ford, two films with director James Cruze, *Mister Skitch* (1933) and *David Harum* (1934), and *Life Begins at Forty* (1934), among others. Many of these were family comedy-dramas set in small-town America, featuring Rogers' popular cracker-barrel philosophizing. His last film was another massive hit with John Ford, *Steamboat Round the Bend* (1935).

Of Hollywood's male stars, Clark Gable was second in popularity only to Will Rogers in 1934 and 1935. By 1936 he was second to none, a position he maintained for the next three years. As Gable said, "the only reason they come to see me is that I know life is great – and they know I know it". Well, hardly the only reason, but it was certainly integral to his popularity. The late thirties were undoubtedly his greatest period. He had just won an Oscar for his performance in Frank Capra's classic comedy *It Happened One Night* (1934),

THE MALE QUIGLEY POLLS

1930	WILLIAM HAINES
1931/32	CHARLES FARRELL
1933-35	WILL ROGERS
1936-38	CLARK GABLE
1939-41	MICKEY ROONEY
1942	ABBOTT AND COSTELLO
1943	BOB HOPE
1944-48	BING CROSBY
1949	BOB HOPE
1950/51	JOHN WAYNE
1952	DEAN MARTIN AND JERRY LEWIS
1953	GARY COOPER
1954	JOHN WAYNE
1955	JAMES STEWART
1956	WILLIAM HOLDEN
1957	ROCK HUDSON
1958	GLENN FORD
1959-62	ROCK HUDSON
1963	JOHN WAYNE
1964	JACK LEMMON
1965/66	SEAN CONNERY
1967	LEE MARVIN
1968	SIDNEY POITIER
1969/70	PAUL NEWMAN
1971	JOHN WAYNE
1972/73	CLINT EASTWOOD
1974-76	ROBERT REDFORD
1977	SYLVESTER STALLONE
1978-82	BURT REYNOLDS
1983/84	CLINT EASTWOOD
1985	SYLVESTER STALLONE
1986	TOM CRUISE
1987	EDDIE MURPHY
1988	TOM CRUISE
1989	JACK NICHOLSON
1990	ARNOLD SCHWARZENEGGER

The first musical MGM produced and won the year's best Picture Oscar for, was the backstage movie *Broadway Melody* (1929). (*The Jazz Singer* (1927) which preceded it did have songs but was not considered a genuine musical.) The "All Talking! All Singing! All Dancing!" production opened on 1 February 1929. MGM later followed this success with three more *Broadway Melody* movies throughout the thirties, and by the early forties was Hollywood's leading producer of musicals, proving the most productive studio for the talents of Fred Astaire, Judy Garland, Gene Kelly, Vincente Minnelli *et al*. The best of these were produced by lyricist Arthur Freed.

was the perfect Fletcher Christian in *Mutiny on the Bounty* (1935) and was starring in a successful series of films with platinum blonde Jean Harlow. Their teaming ended with the disappointing *Saratoga* (1937), when Harlow died from uremic poisoning during production. Gable's biggest hit during this period was *San Francisco* (1936), followed by the popular *Test Pilot*, where he received sterling support from frequent partners Myrna Loy and Spencer Tracy. Loy also starred opposite Gable in *Wife versus Secretary* (1936) and *Too Hot to Handle* (1938), as well as in his biggest flop, the historical drama *Parnell* (1937), based on the life of the 19th-century Irish politician. However, this was not enough to dent Gable's drawing-power at the box-office; surprisingly, he was knocked off the top in 1939, the year of his most enduring success, *Gone with the Wind*.

Taking his place was another MGM star, diminutive 5ft 3in (1m 60cm) Mickey Rooney, who was only 18. Despite his youth, the cocky, exuberant Rooney had been in films for 13 years, making his debut as Mickey McGuire, but it was the Andy Hardy series that made him a massive star. The series began in 1937 with *A Family Affair*. Their appeal was similar to the Will Rogers films; they were reassuring, small-town American family dramas. The series ran for 15 movies and 11 years, winning a special Oscar in 1942 for "representing the American way of life". Rooney was the undoubted star, but first-rate support was provided by Lewis Stone (father, with whom he always had a "man-to-man talk"), Fay Holden (mother), Sara Haden (aunt), Cecilia Parker (sister) and Ann Rutherford (Polly, Andy's most frequent girlfriend). The Hardy films also provided work for a succession of starlets as rivals to Polly for Andy's affections, including Lana Turner, Esther Williams and Judy Garland. Garland and Rooney were also paired in a series of "putting-on-a-show" musicals, usually directed by Busby Berkeley, which were filmed concurrent with the Hardy movies. The first, *Babes in Arms* (1939), was followed by *Strike Up the Band* (1940), *Babes on Broadway* (1941) and *Girl Crazy* (1943). In all, they appeared 10 times together. Rooney's other major successes of the period were *Boys' Town* (1938), for which he won a special Oscar, and *The Adventures of Huckleberry Finn* (1939). But he became typecast – "I played 14-year-old boys for 30 years" – and after the war never regained the same popularity. Nevertheless, he continued to entertain audiences in films as diverse as Rouben Mamoulian's musical *Summer Holiday* (1948), the war movie *The Bold and the Brave* (1958), for which he won an Oscar nomination, the gangster movie *Baby Face Nelson* (1957) and Disney's part-animated *Pete's Dragon* (1977).

The male box-office kings of the forties were mostly comedians or, in the case of Bing Crosby, actors who were often starred in comedies. Dominating the Quigley poll between 1943 and 1949 were Paramount stars Bob Hope and Bing Crosby. However, in 1942 burlesque and radio stars Abbott and Costello were top of the heap. They made seven films over two years in 1941 and 1942, with almost interchangeable titles like *In the Navy* (1941), *Keep 'em Flying* (1941) and *Ride 'em Cowboy* (1941). Only *Hold That Ghost* (1941) remains particularly enjoyable today. They churned films out at a rate of approximately two a year until 1956, appearing in the

Quigley top 10 on eight occasions.

Although not strictly a team in the same manner as Abbott and Costello, Hope and Crosby starred in seven popular "Road" movies as double-crossing partners chasing Dorothy Lamour, often using their famous "patty-cake" routine to get out of the inevitable trouble. The best of the series – *Road to Morocco* (1942), *Road to Utopia* (1945) and *Road to Rio* (1947) – appeared in the mid-forties. Hope and Crosby were also equally successful apart. The wisecracking, cowardly Hope scored his biggest hit of the decade opposite Jane Russell in the western spoof *The Paleface* (1948), as the dentist Painless Potter singing the Oscar-winning "Buttons and Bows". A sequel, *Son of Paleface* (1952), followed four years later. Hope's other successes included the horror-comedies, *The Cat and the Canary* (1939) and *The Ghost Breakers* (1940), and further films with Dorothy Lamour, the best being the spy-comedy *They Got Me Covered* (1943). He also had big hits with period comedies *The Princess and the Pirate* (1944) and *Monsieur Beaucaire* (1946).

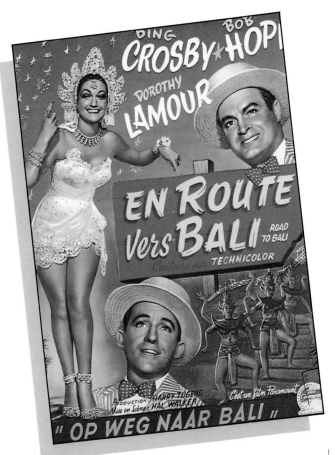

Bing Crosby was even more popular, winning an Oscar for his performance as Father O'Malley in the sentimental *Going My Way* (1944), in which he was teamed with Barry Fitzgerald and crooned a couple of songs. The result was dynamite at the box-office. Naturally, Crosby and Fitzgerald teamed up again in *Welcome Stranger* (1947) and *Top o' the Morning* (1949), and Father O'Malley put in another appearance in the even more successful *The Bells of St Mary's* (1945). Two movies with the great Fred Astaire, particularly *Holiday Inn* (1942) in which Crosby sang "White Christmas", further enhanced his standing. He remained in the top 10 until 1954, the year he won an Oscar nomination for his dramatic characterization of an alcoholic singer in *The Country Girl* (1954). Crosby's appeal lies in his apparently easy-going, self-effacing ordinariness, which he clearly understood. "He

ABOVE Bud Abbott and Lou Costello, the forties most popular comedy team churned out films at a rate of about two per year.

LEFT Hope, Crosby and Lamour, Paramount's popular trio in *Road to Bali*, the first "Road" movie to be made in colour.

RIGHT *Strike Up the Band*, featuring the incomparable Mickey Rooney and Judy Garland, Hollywood's best child-performers during the late thirties and early forties.

RIGHT A young Bing Crosby; box-office king of the forties. He won an Oscar for his performance in *Going My Way* in 1944.

was an average guy who could carry a tune," he said of himself, and he earned over $300,000 a year during the war for doing so.

By contrast, the fifties was dominated by men of action, the notable exception being the comedy team of Dean Martin and Jerry Lewis, who remained in Quigley's top 10 until the act broke up in 1956. Their 16 titles are as indistinguishable as Abbott and Costello's and included *At War With the Army* (1951), *Sailor Beware* (1952) and *Scared Stiff* (1953). Both did their best work separately; Martin opposite John Wayne in the Howard Hawks western *Rio Bravo* (1959) and co-starring with Kim Novak in the neglected Billy Wilder comedy *Kiss Me Stupid* (1964); Lewis in the Dr Jekyll and Mr Hyde-based comedy *The Nutty Professor* (1963) and as television chat-show host Jerry Langford in Martin Scorsese's brilliant, bleak, commercial failure *King of Comedy* (1982).

The most durable star must be John Wayne, who has appeared in Quigley's top 10 box-office stars a record 25 times between 1949 and 1974. Wayne's career is inextricably linked with director John Ford and the western. Their first teaming is probably their most famous, *Stagecoach* (1939), with Wayne perfectly cast as the Ringo Kid, although *The*

ABOVE "The girls call me Pilgrim because every time I dance with one I make a little progress," was typical Bob Hope patter.

LEFT Dean Martin and Jerry Lewis, who made 16 movies together, seen here in the western spoof *Pardners* (1956).

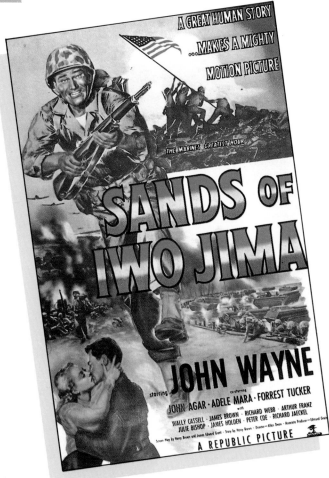

The Green Berets (1968), have at times overshadowed the richness of his best movies and performances.

Gary Cooper also has strong links with the western and became the leading box-office star of 1953 on the strength of Fred Zinnemann's *High Noon* (1952), which earned nearly $3.5 million and won Cooper a second Oscar for his performance as Marshall Will Kane, who stands alone against four gunslingers. Another western, *Distant Drums* (1951), was also a big hit during this period. However, Cooper made more varied movies earlier in his career, with Rouben Mamoulian's gangster drama *City Streets* (1931), the classic weepie *A Farewell to Arms* (1932), based on Ernest Hemingway's novel, Ernst Lubitsch comedies *Design for Living* (1933) and *Desire* (1936), and Frank Capra comedies *Mr Deeds Goes to Town* (1936) and *Meet John Doe* (1941). The forties began with two good Howard Hawks movies, *The Westerner* (1940) and *Sergeant York* (1941), for which he won his first Oscar. Gary Cooper remained a star until his death from cancer in 1961, winning a special Oscar in 1960 "for his many memor-

ABOVE *Sands of Iwo Jima*, the film for which John Wayne gained his first Oscar nomination.

RIGHT "I've never had a goddam artistic problem in my life, never, and I've worked with the best of them. John Ford isn't exactly a bum, is he? Yet he never gave me any manure about art." – The Duke.

Searchers (1956) is undoubtedly the most rewarding and *The Man Who Shot Liberty Valance* (1962) the most undervalued. Other notable Ford-Wayne successes include the war movie *They Were Expendable* (1945), the cavalry movie *She Wore a Yellow Ribbon* (1949) and the Irish comedy *The Quiet Man* (1952). Wayne's work with director Howard Hawks was also particularly rewarding, notably in the westerns *Red River* (1948) and *Rio Bravo*. The latter made over $5,000,000 and was rehashed by Wayne and Hawks as *El Dorado* (1966), which made even more money. Oddly, the Academy of Motion Picture Arts and Sciences chose to honour Wayne at Oscar time for two less distinguished movies. His performance in *Sands of Iwo Jima* (1949) earned him his first Oscar nomination, presumably for agreeing to die at the film's climax. He finally won the Best Actor Oscar for playing ageing, one-eyed marshall, Reuben J "Rooster" Cogburn in *True Grit* (1969). Regrettably, Wayne's simplistic patriotism and right-wing politics, displayed in movies like the crude Communist-bashing *Big Jim McLain* (1952) and the Vietnam war-movie

able screen performances and for the international recognition he, as an individual, has gained for the film industry". However, he seemed to have been insecure about his acting abilities, telling fellow actor Jeff Corey, "I only have two or three tricks, and that's not enough, is it?" Cooper claimed simply to consider himself "Mr Average Joe American", and, while he patently wasn't, this seems to be the essence of his enduring popularity.

Perhaps even more respected was James Stewart, who rose to fame in some excellent comedies during the late thirties. He was especially successful in those of Frank Capra, *You Can't Take it With You* (1938), *Mr Smith Goes to Washington* (1939) and, Stewart's own favourite, *It's a Wonderful Life* (1946), although this, surprisingly, was not a hit on release. It was during this period that Stewart won an Oscar for his performance alongside Cary Grant and Katharine Hepburn in George Cukor's *The Philadelphia Story* (1940). He always seemed to play fully rounded characters, whether in his early comedy hits or the series of westerns he made with director

LEFT A much younger Gary Cooper, aged 34 in 1934 when he still made films other than westerns.

BELOW Gary Cooper in his best-remembered movie, Fred Zinnemann's *High Noon*, for which he won an Oscar and Golden Globe.

ABOVE Fritz Lang's *The Big Heat* (1953), starring Glenn Ford and Gloria Grahame. The following year the same trio made *Human Desire.*

Anthony Mann in the fifties. These Mann westerns usually featured lead characters tormented by their past, frequently driven to violence, and made superb use of landscape. The first two, *Winchester 73* (1950) and *Bend of the River* (1952; *Where the River Bends*), were big hits and therefore were followed by *The Naked Spur* (1952), *The Far Country* (1954) and, their best collaboration, *The Man From Laramie* (1955). Stewart was also fortunate to work with Hitchcock, in *Rear Window* (1954), *The Man Who Knew Too Much* (1956) and *Vertigo* (1958), and with Billy Wilder, in the story of Charles Lindburgh, *The Spirit of St Louis* (1957). His pairing with June Allyson in two big hits, *The Glenn Miller Story* (1954) and *Strategic Air Command* (1955), both directed by Mann, further enhanced his box-office pull. His star power has never really diminished, only his films.

Both William Holden and Glenn Ford also had careers stretching over 30 years, but lacked the charisma of Stewart, Cooper and Wayne, despite starring in fine movies like *Sunset*

Boulevard (1950) and *Gilda* (1946) respectively. Holden was top box-office star of 1956 through appearing in two successful movies, the tear-jerker *Love is a Many Splendoured Thing* (1955) and the small-town melodrama *Picnic* (1956), while Ford gave his best performance as the charming outlaw in Delmer Daves' fine western *3.10 to Yuma* (1957). Ford also starred in two big hits during the mid-fifties, the comedies *The Teahouse of the August Moon* (1956) opposite Marlon Brando and *Don't Go Near the Water* (1957).

Like many of the top box-office stars, Rock Hudson was equally at home in action movies or comedies. He was also noted for some excellent melodramas, often playing the dependable, immovable character in a film. But then, as Hudson knew, "I can't play a loser – I don't look like one". He considered his best movie to be George Stevens' *Giant* (1956), which won him an Oscar nomination. However, it seems particularly stolid next to the movies he made with Douglas Sirk, whom Hudson was later to claim "was the first

ABOVE According to Bette Davis "he is one of our most beloved stars," and in 1985 James Stewart, seen here in Anthony Mann's *Thunder Bay* (1953), was awarded an honorary Oscar.

FAR LEFT William Holden, who began his film career with *Golden Boy* in 1939, reached his peak in the fifties.

LEFT Rock Hudson's studio-arranged marriage to Phyllis Gates on 9 November 1955.

good director I worked with". The quartet of classic melodramas Sirk and Hudson made together are *Magnificent Obsession* (1954), *All That Heaven Allows* (1955), which was their best and a fine critique of conformist small-town America, *Written on the Wind* (1956) and *The Tarnished Angels* (1957). They also worked together on musicals including *Has Anybody Seen My Gal?* (1952), westerns such as *Taza, Son of Cochise* (1954), and biopics, for instance *Battle Hymn* (1957). As the fifties drew to a close Hudson changed direction, making a series of lightweight comedies. His most popular co-star was Doris Day, who was the top female star during the same period, and they appeared together in *Pillow Talk* (1959), *Lover Come Back* (1961) and *Send Me No Flowers* (1964). However, despite their popularity at the time, the "sophisticated sex comedies" have faded compared with the Sirk melodramas.

ABOVE Jack Lemmon (left) and Edward G Robinson in the comedy *The Good Neighbour Sam* (1964).

RIGHT "If you were his friend in those days, you didn't mention the subject of Bond ever." – Michael Caine said of Sean Connery.

The sixties seemed to have a different actor proving most popular each year. There was Jack Lemmon, who was then acting in comedies, such as the Billy Wilder movies *Irma La Douce* (1963) and *The Fortune Cookie* (1966; *Meet Whiplash Willie*), *How to Murder Your Wife* (1964), ably supported by Terry Thomas and Eddie Mayehoff, and the lavish *The Great Race* (1965) as well as other films. He later proved equally at ease in serious roles, such as *The China Syndrome* (1979) and *Missing* (1982). Sean Connery reached the peak of his box-office power in the mid-sixties with the best of the Bond movies – *From Russia with Love* (1963) and *Goldfinger* (1964) – as well as flexing his acting muscles in Hitchcock's *Marnie* (1964) and Sidney Lumet's *The Hill* (1965). In 1983 he was still considered worth $5 million to reprise the Bond role in *Never Say Never Again*, while seven years later Spielberg stated that "there are only seven genuine film stars in the world today" – Sean Connery was naturally still one of them.

Lee Marvin graduated from first-rate heavy to star with the western comedy *Cat Ballou* (1965) and consolidated his position as the leading male star with *The Professionals* (1966) opposite Burt Lancaster, the all-star war movie *The Dirty Dozen* (1967) and John Boorman's excellent gangster film *Point Blank* (1967). Boorman had been drawn by what he described as an "unpredictable, explosive violence that was modified by an exhilarating eloquence". And Sidney Poitier became the first black actor to top the Quigley poll, winning an Oscar for *Lilies of the Field* in 1963 and starring in

LEFT & BOTTOM LEFT
Sean Connery and Ursula Andress in the highly successful *Dr No*.

BELOW Connery was tempted back as Bond for *Diamonds Are Forever*, but only for a fee of $1,2 million which he presented to the Scottish International Educational Trust.

RIGHT Sidney Poitier, seen with Katharine Hepburn and Spencer Tracy in their last film together, *Guess Who's Coming to Dinner?*.

BELOW Paul Newman, here with Tom Cruise, repeated his role as Fast Eddie Felson from *The Hustler* in Martin Scorsese's *The Color of Money* and won his first Oscar ever.

the popular *In the Heat of the Night* (1967) and *Guess Who's Coming to Dinner?* (1967). In both films the central issue was the colour of his skin. In fact, it was all too rare for Poitier to be cast in a role where it wasn't.

The three male stars dominating from the late sixties to the mid-seventies were Paul Newman, Clint Eastwood and Steve McQueen, although surprisingly McQueen never headed the poll. Paul Newman has maintained a position at the top since the mid-fifties with the perfect balance of fine acting and star charisma. Following his debut in *The Silver Chalice* (1955), which Newman frequently refers to as "the worst film of the fifties", he made a strong impression as boxer Rocky Graziano in *Somebody Up There Likes Me* (1956), in the excellent melo-drama *The Long, Hot Summer* (1958), in Tennessee Williams' *Cat on a Hot Tin Roof* (1958), as ace pool player Fast Eddie Felson in *The Hustler* (1961) and in the title role of *Hud*

LEFT Robert Redford teamed with top female star Barbra Streisand for *The Way We Were*. The film made $22 million at the North American box-office.

BELOW Initially Clint Eastwood spoke no Italian and Italian director Sergio Leone spoke no English, making communication on the first of the "Dollar" movies a little difficult.

(1963). He also partnered his wife, Joanne Woodward, in 10 movies of variable quality. His career seemed to have peaked by the late sixties, until he was teamed with Robert Redford for the comedy western *Butch Cassidy and the Sundance Kid* (1969). The film was a smash, as was their subsequent teaming in *The Sting* (1973). Newman remained a big star in the eighties, finally winning an Oscar for his second performance as Fast Eddie in *The Color of Money* (1986), and playing Governor Earl K Long in the underrated *Blaze* (1990). But he seems slightly dissatisfied with his films, claiming in 1987 that "I haven't liked much of the work I've done in the past 25 years". If he hasn't quite lived up to the promise of the early sixties, that's only because the promise was so great.

Eastwood has skilfully juggled his career, alternating between starring roles in cop movies like the Dirty Harry series and directing his own more personal films, for instance the

RIGHT Steve McQueen in *Papillon*; he was a big star during the sixties, but never managed to head the Quigley Poll.

BELOW Sylvester Stallone in the third instalment of the rags-to-riches boxing saga *Rocky*, here with Mr T, his opponent.

gentle, Capraesque comedy *Bronco Billy* (1980) and the Charlie Parker biopic *Bird* (1988). The 6ft 4in (1m 93cm) Eastwood made his name in westerns, first on television with *Rawhide* (1958-65) and then as the unshaven anti-hero of few words in the spaghetti westerns of Sergio Leone, for whom he made the hugely successful Dollars movies. *A Fistful of Dollars* (1964), *For a Few Dollars More* (1965) and *The Good, the Bad and the Ugly* (1966) made Eastwood an international star. They also revitalized the genre. He maintained his star status on returning to America, particularly through his collaborations with director Don Siegel in the cop thrillers *Coogan's Bluff* (1968) and *Dirty Harry* (1971), as well as the off-beat *The Beguiled* (1971). Siegel felt "the hardest thing in the world is to do nothing and he does it marvellously", while Richard Burton, his co-star in *Where Eagles Dare* (1969), compared him to Spencer Tracy and Robert Mitchum.

Eastwood's position as Hollywood's most bankable star was stolen by Robert Redford, Paul Newman's co-star from *Butch Cassidy and the Sundance Kid*. Redford made a series of thoughtful yet slightly dull movies, often with a liberal slant, such as the western *Tell Them Willie Boy is Here* (1969), the political drama *The Candidate* (1972), *The Way We Were* (1973) in which he was teamed with Barbra Streisand, *The Sting* and *The Great Waldo Pepper* (1975). Like their star, these films looked good but seemed to lack passion. His best during this period was probably *Jeremiah Johnson* (1972), in which he played a trapper living in isolation in the mountains, although *All the President's Men* (1976), based on the Watergate scandal, is reasonably compelling. Despite these criticisms, Redford's movies are instantly preferable to either Stallone's or Reynolds'.

Stallone shot to fame using the underdog boxer cliché in *Rocky* (1976) and then proceeded to milk the formula dry on four more occasions. Stallone's other enduring character was Vietnam veteran John Rambo, originally in the dull *First Blood* (1982), where he comes up against a small-town sheriff (played by the ever-excellent Brian Dennehy), and then in *Rambo: First Blood Part Two* (1985), where he returns to Vietnam to rescue American prisoners. By the time of *Rambo III* (1988) he was sent to Afghanistan to kick hell out of the Russkies. Stallone was the first star to be considered worth $10 million for one movie.

At least Reynolds has made some good movies in John Boorman's *Deliverance* (1972), pitted against the hostile environment of the Appalachian mountains and their hillbilly dwellers, the neglected private eye movie *Shamus* (1972) and Robert Aldrich's *Hustle* (1975), but these came before the peak of his popularity. This coincided with the dire *Smokey and the Bandit* series and the *Cannonball Run* movies, which centred on Reynolds' broad grin, the destruction of a vast number of cars and endless attempts to prove that the word "shit" is somehow intrinsically funny. Nevertheless, Reynolds was able to command a fee of $5 million plus percentage for playing the lead in *The Cannonball Run* (1980), which must have eased the pain of being typecast a little.

The late eighties saw almost as much variety as the sixties. Tom Cruise made his name in teen comedies, having most success with *Risky Business* (1983), before trying to prove

himself a real actor with Paul Newman in *The Color of Money*, with Dustin Hoffman in *Rain Man* (1988) and as Vietnam veteran Ron Kovic in Oliver Stone's *Born on the Fourth of July* (1989). Eddie Murphy came to prominence with a number of comedy hits, the best being his first, *Trading Places* (1983). Nevertheless, the routine *Beverly Hills Cop* (1984) was among the top 10 hits of the eighties and the dire *The Golden Child* (1986), *Coming to America* (1988) and *Beverly Hills Cop II* (1987) all inexplicably made large amounts of money.

Jack Nicholson had been a leading star-cum-actor for many years before topping the Quigley poll. Throughout the sixties and seventies he starred in some excellent movies, from early Corman low-budget projects to two excellent Bob Rafelson dramas, *Five Easy Pieces* (1970) and *The King of Marvin Gardens* (1972), and also *The Last Detail* (1973) and

ABOVE Tom Cruise and Kelly McGillis in Tony Scott's slick movie *Top Gun*. Cruise made his name mainly in teen comedies.

RIGHT Jack Nicholson at his peak, as private eye J J Gittes in Roman Polanski's *Chinatown* with Faye Dunaway.

Polanski's superb thirties private detective mystery, *China-town* (1974). Nicholson later gave an Oscar-winning performance in *One Flew Over the Cuckoo's Nest* (1975). He finally made it to the top of the box-office pile following the dull melodramas *Terms of Endearment* (1983) and *Heartburn* (1986), starring as The Devil ("A lot of people think I've been preparing for it all my life") in the overblown *The Witches of Eastwick* (1987) and in a highly overrated performance as The Joker in *Batman* (1989), for which he is rumoured to have been paid over $50 million.

The current top star, Arnold Schwarzenegger, is not likely to go hungry either, earning $15 million for *Terminator 2: Judgment Day* (1991; see page 50). Schwarzenegger has been seen to best effect in science fiction movies, such as *The Terminator* (1984), *Predator* (1987) and *Total Recall* (1990). However, he seems to have learnt the lesson of the more enduring stars of the past and branched out into comedy with *Twins* (1988) and *Kindergarten Cop* (1990), neither particularly good movies but popular nevertheless. Given the stunning success of *Terminator 2*, he looks set to be around for a while yet.

★ NOTABLE FIRST ★

The first talking feature was *The Jazz Singer* (1927), produced by the struggling Warner Brothers and premiered on 6 October 1927 at the Warner Theater in New York. Warners, particularly Sam Warner, had been encouraged by the critics' response to *Don Juan* (1926), which had been released with a synchronized soundtrack. *The Jazz Singer*'s original lead, George Jessel, demanded too much money and was rejected in favour of Al Jolson, a bigger star. Jolson introduced dialogue to the feature film with his famous ad-libbed speech "Wait a minute, wait a minute, you ain't heard nothing yet", as well as performing songs like "Mammy" and Irving Berlin's "Blue Skies". *The Jazz Singer*'s success led Hollywood's other major studios to turn to sound, resulting in panic over the suitability of their leading star's voices. The success was marred for the brothers when Sam Warner died of a cerebral haemorrhage 24 hours before the premiere.

TOP LEFT Eddie Murphy became a top box-office star with a string of routine comedies.

ABOVE Jack Nicholson as not-so-bright hitman Charley Partanna in John Huston's *Prizzi's Honour.*

TOP BOX-OFFICE FEMALE STARS

Both the oldest (Marie Dressler) and the youngest (Shirley Temple) stars to top the Quigley poll came in the thirties, with Janet Gaynor sandwiched in between. Before them came MGM star Joan Crawford, at the height of her flapper-girl popularity in films like *Untamed* (1929) and *Our Blushing Brides* (1930). Her best-remembered work, melodramas of the calibre of *Mildred Pierce* (1945) and *Humoresque* (1946), were still many years away.

BELOW The popular Janet Gaynor and Charles Farrell in *Street Angel*, one of 12 teamings.

LEFT Janet Gaynor, voted top box-office female star in 1934 by the Quigley Poll.

Gaynor and the films she made with the equally popular Charles Farrell (see pages 60-61) have been generally neglected, despite her winning the first Best Actress Oscar for her performances in *Seventh Heaven* (1927), *Street Angel* (1928) and F W Murnau's classic silent movie *Sunrise* (1927). The first two were both made with Farrell and director Frank Borzage. Apart from *Sunrise*, she scored successes away from Farrell with *Daddy Longlegs* (1931), with top male box-office star Will Rogers in *State Fair* (1933) and in the first version of *A Star is Born* (1937), as aspiring actress Esther Blodgett who becomes a star as Vicki Lester, a role that brought another Oscar nomination.

MGM star Marie Dressler has to be one of Hollywood's most unlikely stars, her most successful period coming in her sixties. Like her elderly male contemporary Will Rogers, her reign as box-office queen was ended only by death, on 28 July 1934 from cancer. Dressler made her debut opposite Charlie Chaplin in *Tillie's Punctured Romance* (1914), but it wasn't until 1930 that she became a major star after appearing in Greta Garbo's talkie debut *Anna Christie* and playing opposite

LEFT Marie Dressler and Wallace Beery in *Min and Bill* earned $2 miillion for MGM.

Wallace Beery in the comedy *Min and Bill*. The latter won her an Oscar and led to a similar reteaming in *Tugboat Annie* (1933). Both Dressler-Beery films were among the top 15 box-office hits of their year, as were the comedies *Reducing* (1931) and *Politics* (1931), both with frequent co-star Polly Moran, and the drama *Emma* (1932), for which she won an Oscar nomination.

The 64-year-old Dressler's place was filled by seven-year-old Shirley Temple. Temple made her feature debut aged four in *Red-Haired Alibi* (1932), following a number of Baby Burlesk shorts, and won a special Oscar only two years later "in grateful recognition of her outstanding contribution to screen entertainment during the year 1934". By 1938 she was earning over $300,000 a year, as well as having been named an honorary G-Man by J Edgar Hoover. Fox's biggest star appeared in a string of well-crafted, tailor-made vehicles with titles like *Heidi* (1937), *Bright Eyes* (1934) and *Curly Top*

THE FEMALE QUIGLEY POLL

1930	JOAN CRAWFORD
1931-33	MARIE DRESSLER
1934	JANET GAYNOR
1935-39	SHIRLEY TEMPLE
1940/41	BETTE DAVIS
1942-44	BETTY GRABLE
1945	GREER GARSON
1946	INGRID BERGMAN
1947-51	BETTY GRABLE
1952	DORIS DAY
1953-54	MARILYN MONROE
1955	GRACE KELLY
1956	MARILYN MONROE
1957	KIM NOVAK
1956	ELIZABETH TAYLOR
1959/60	DORIS DAY
1961	ELIZABETH TAYLOR
1962-65	DORIS DAY
1966-68	JULIE ANDREWS
1969	KATHARINE HEPBURN
1970	BARBRA STREISAND
1971	ALI McGRAW
1972-75	BARBRA STREISAND
1976	TATUM O'NEAL
1977	BARBRA STREISAND
1978	DIANE KEATON
1979/80	JANE FONDA
1981/82	DOLLY PARTON
1983	MERYL STREEP
1984	SALLY FIELD
1985	MERYL STREEP
1986	BETTE MIDLER
1987	GLENN CLOSE
1988	BETTE MIDLER
1989	KATHLEEN TURNER
1990	JULIA ROBERTS

ABOVE Shirley Temple, the most popular star of the thirties, at one time had 4 million members in her fan club.

TOP RIGHT Betty Grable in *Wabash Avenue*, a remake of her earlier hit *Coney Island*. First-rate support was provided by Victor Mature, Phil Harris, Reginald Gardiner and Margaret Hamilton.

(1935) Their appeal today depends almost solely on how much of Shirley Temple an audience can take. Nevertheless, she worked with some top talent, such as Gary Cooper and Carole Lombard in *Now and Forever* (1934), Lionel Barrymore in *The Little Colonel* (1935), Joel McCrea in *Our Little Girl* (1935), Bill Robinson in *The Littlest Rebel* (1935), Frank Morgan in *Dimples* (1936), director John Ford in *Wee Willie Winkie* (1937) and so on. Her star status declined after playing the lead in Fox's expensive fantasy *The Blue Bird* (1940), which compared badly with *The Wizard of Oz* (1939), and she never made the tricky transition from child to adult star. Instead, she retired from the screen and later went into politics, a little disillusioned: "I stopped believing in Santa Claus when I was six. Mother took me to see him in a department store and he asked me for my autograph." Nevertheless she should be credited for her many successes.

The forties was dominated by one performer, the forces' pin-up Betty Grable, who starred in a series of lightweight musicals for Twentieth Century-Fox. Grable had been in movies since 1930, either in supporting roles such as the Astaire-Rogers musicals *The Gay Divorcée* (1934; *The Gay Divorce*) and *Follow the Fleet* (1936) or starring in minor films like the aptly titled *Million Dollar Legs* (1939), the sum her famous assets were later insured for with Lloyds of London. Her career really took off with *Down Argentine Way* (1940), when she took over the leading role from Fox's top musical star of the era, Alice Faye, who had appendicitis. The film also starred Brazilian bombshell Carmen Miranda in her Hollywood debut and the underrated Don Ameche. The successful *Down Argentine Way* was followed by *Tin Pan Alley* (1940), in which Grable was teamed with Faye, and *Moon Over Miami* (1941), again with Ameche. She was the top

LEFT "William Wylder was and always will be the greatest director Hollywood ever had." Bette Davis in William Wyler's *The Little Foxes*.

female box-office star for most of the forties, receiving 10,000 fan letters a week and starring in a series of indistinguishable films like *Coney Island* (1943), *Sweet Rosie O'Grady* (1943), *Pin-Up Girl* (1944), *The Dolly Sisters* (1945), *Wabash Avenue* (1950; a remake of *Coney Island*) and *My Blue Heaven* (1950). She was fortunate that her cheerful personality and limited talent was backed by some of Hollywood's best supporting performers: Jack Oakie, Allen Jenkins, Jack Haley, the Nicholas Brothers, Thomas Mitchell, Billy Gilbert, Edward Everett Horton, Adolphe Menjou and the incomparable Phil Silvers, to name but a few.

Fortunately the forties provided more than Betty Grable. As the decade began Bette Davis was hitting her finest patch, following the great melodramatic excesses of *Jezebel* (1938), *Dark Victory* (1939) and *The Old Maid* (1939). The early forties saw the quality of the melodramas improve even further,

starting with William Wyler's adaptation of W Somerset Maugham's *The Letter* (1940) and followed by another Wyler film, the superb *The Little Foxes* (1941) and, perhaps Davis' best-loved film, the classic tear-jerker *Now Voyager* (1942). Her appeal is best summed up by the advertising for the John Huston melodrama *In This Our Life* (1942): "Nobody is as good as Bette when she's bad!" it rightly claimed. Davis was also seen at her most likeable in the wonderful comedy *The Man Who Came to Dinner* (1941), even managing to hold her own alongside Monty Woolley, Jimmy Durante and Reginald Gardiner. It's a pity she wasn't given more comedy roles. Davis' best period may have been over by the mid-forties, but she was still earning $365,000 a year in 1948 and her Oscar-nominated performances in *All About Eve* (1950) and *Whatever Happened to Baby Jane?* (1962) were yet to come. All this from an actress whom Universal boss Carl Laemmle had dismissed as having "as much sex appeal as Slim Summerville".

Greer Garson and Ingrid Bergman also reigned briefly as the top female box-office stars, the red-headed Garson through the classic weepie *Random Harvest* (1942) and a series of eight dramas with Walter Pidgeon, including *Mrs Miniver* (1942), *Madame Curie* (1943) and *Mrs Parkington* (1944). The Swedish Bergman reached her peak in the mid-forties. She co-starred with Bogart in *Casablanca* (1942), Cooper in *For Whom the Bell Tolls* (1943), Crosby in *The Bells of St Mary's* (1945) and won an Oscar for *Gaslight* (1944; *The Murder in Thornton Square*), as well as starring in two Hitchcock classics, *Spellbound* (1945) and *Notorious* (1946). Unfortunately her Hollywood career was killed by her affair with Italian director Roberto Rossellini in 1949, which received much adverse publicity when she decided to have his child.

The fifties was undoubtedly the decade of the blonde, be she virginal (Doris Day), sexual (Marilyn Monroe) or ice-cool (Grace Kelly and Kim Novak). Doris Day had the longest career of the quartet, having been ranked the most popular female star for the first time in 1952, a position she could still claim 13 years later. Her career is usually divided into the energetic musicals of the fifties, typified by *Calamity Jane* (1953), and the glossy yet empty comedies of the sixties, best represented by her three films with Rock Hudson. But there is slightly more of interest, including the good Ku-Klux-Klan drama *Storm Warning* (1950), the two enjoyable turn-of-the-

BELOW An amnesiac Ronald Colman as "Smithy" falls for Greer Garson's music-hall singer Paula in the classic weepie *Random Harvest*.

TOP LEFT Ingrid Bergman's performance in *Joan of Arc* earned her an Oscar nomination.

TOP RIGHT Doris Day and Howard Keel, just blown in from the windy city, in *Calamity Jane*.

LEFT Doris Day in *On Moonlight Bay*, among the best of her fifties musicals, despite the obvious comparisons with *Meet Me in St Louis*.

RIGHT Marilyn Monroe in *Gentlemen Prefer Blondes*, although Jane Russell might not agree.

BELOW A rare colour shot from *Some Like It Hot*; the radiant Sugar Kane (Marilyn Monroe) with Daphne (Jack Lemmon).

ABOVE Marilyn Monroe filming Billy Wilder's *The Seven Year Itch*.

century family musicals *On Moonlight Bay* (1951) and *By the Light of the Silvery Moon* (1953), which were obviously inspired by the superior *Meet Me in St Louis* (1944), the music drama *Young at Heart* (1954) opposite Frank Sinatra, and the Ruth Etting biopic *Love Me or Leave Me* (1955) with James Cagney, a Hitchcock movie, his second version of *The Man Who Knew Too Much* (1956), and the likeable newspaper comedy *Teacher's Pet* (1957) with Clark Gable. When cinema audiences lost interest in the mid-sixties she turned to television with *The Doris Day Show* (1968-72).

Marilyn Monroe never had the opportunity to tailor her talents to the changing tastes of the sixties. She died in 1962, and her death has since been the subject of much debate and controversy. In fact, it has received more attention than her films, as have her marriages to Joe DiMaggio and Arthur Miller, her miscarriages, her problems on set, and her famous quotes. Surprisingly, Monroe was ranked number one female star only once, in 1956, when her best movies were still to come. Following good supporting roles in *The Asphalt Jungle* (1950) and *All About Eve*, she appeared in a number of flaccid comedies and musicals, such as *Gentlemen Prefer Blondes* (1953) and *How to Marry a Millionaire* (1953). Her best films came towards the end of her career in Billy Wilder's sparkling *Some Like It Hot* (1959), where she found her perfect role as the sensuous yet vulnerable Sugar Kane, and John Huston's tragic drama of modern cowboys, *The Misfits* (1961). It was the last film she completed.

Grace Kelly's fame was even shorter-lived, her peak crammed into three years between 1954 and 1956, although she had earlier supported Gary Cooper in *High Noon* (1952). Her success is probably due to Alfred Hitchcock, who cast her in *Dial M For Murder* (1954), *Rear Window* (1954) and *To Catch a Thief* (1955). Hitchcock felt that the aloof Kelly fitted his preference for ice-cool blondes: "The drawing-room types, the real ladies, who become whores once they're in the bedroom." Her two other notable roles came opposite Bing Crosby, winning an Oscar for *The Country Girl* (1954) and proving the least interesting part of the popular musical *High Society* (1956). She retired the same year to become Princess Grace of Monaco, which is probably just as well since she seemed to lack the versatility to sustain a lengthy film career. Kim Novak's acting abilities were also limited, but her combination of mystery and vulnerability enabled her to sustain

LEFT Kim Novak, another of Hitchcock's blondes, seen here with James Stewart in *Vertigo*.

her star status until the mid-sixties. She knew her limitations: "I had trained as a model before coming to films, so I had to learn the art of acting right in front of the cameras – while they were turning!" Naturally, Hitchcock chose to work with Novak as well, in the superb *Vertigo* (1958), while she was also seen to good effect in Billy Wilder's *Kiss Me Stupid* (1964).

The top female stars of the sixties were a mixed bag, comprising Elizabeth Taylor, Doris Day, Julie Andrews and Katharine Hepburn. Taylor was one of the few child-actresses to make the successful transition to adult star. She had a big hit as a child with *National Velvet* (1945) and then as an adolescent in *Father of the Bride* (1950). Her adult career seemed assured after her performance opposite Montgomery Clift in *A Place in the Sun* (1951) but only hit its stride five years later

RIGHT Elizabeth Taylor as *Cleopatra*. It may have taken $26 million at the North American box-office, but it cost $44 million to produce.

when she starred opposite Rock Hudson in *Giant* (1956), followed by further teamings with Clift in *Raintree County* (1958) and *Suddenly Last Summer* (1959), and Paul Newman in *Cat on a Hot Tin Roof* (1958). Her fame was seemingly effortlessly maintained throughout the sixties through a combination of her stunning beauty, Oscar-winning performances in *Butterfield 8* (1960), and *Who's Afraid of Virginia Woolf?* (1966) and a highly publicized marriage to, and teaming with Richard Burton in *Cleopatra* (1963).

Despite the media's frequent nostalgic reminiscences about the sexually liberated swinging sixties, virginal Doris Day was replaced as top female star by the equally virginal Julie Andrews, whose reputation seems to rest on two overlong yet hugely popular musicals: *Mary Poppins* (1964) and *The Sound of Music* (1965; see pages 30-31). She was seen to better effect in the comedy *The Americanization of Emily* (1964) with James Garner, and scored another big hit with *Thoroughly Modern Millie* (1967), which took over $8 million. But Andrews' success was short-lived. She had the misfortune to work on one of Hitchcock's lesser movies, *Torn Curtain* (1966), played the lead in the commercially disastrous biopic of Gertrude Lawrence, *Star!* (1968), and appeared in her future husband Blake Edwards' flop *Darling Lili* (1970).

Katharine Hepburn had been both one of Hollywood's leading stars and most respected actresses for many years before being ranked number one. She had starred in dramas such as *Stage Door* (1937) and *Morning Glory* (1933), for which she won an Oscar, the classic Hollywood comedies *Bringing Up Baby* (1938) and *The Philadelphia Story* (1940), a series of movies with her long-time partner Spencer Tracy, and with Humphrey Bogart in the perennial favourite *The African Queen* (1951). Her career seemed to get second wind in the late sixties, when she won Oscars in consecutive years for the dull and patronizing *Guess Who's Coming to Dinner?* (1967), also Spencer Tracy's last film, and *The Lion in Winter* (1968). She was still winning Oscars as late as 1981, for *On Golden Pond*.

The seventies were firmly dominated by Barbra Streisand, one of the few bankable female stars of the era. Regrettably she made few good films. After winning an Oscar for her performance as Fanny Brice in her debut movie, *Funny Girl* (1968), a part she had earlier played on Broadway for two years, Streisand had hits with *The Owl and the Pussycat* (1970),

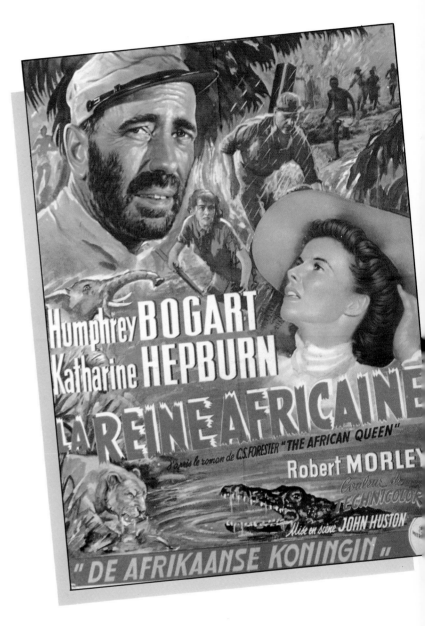

The Way We Were (1973) with the equally bankable Robert Redford, the *Funny Girl* sequel *Funny Lady* (1975) and the third (and worst) version of *A Star is Born* (1976). Her most enjoyable film is Peter Bogdanovich's *What's Up Doc?* (1972), although this also paled when compared to the thirties screwball comedies from which it took its inspiration. *What's Up Doc?* co-star Ryan O'Neal was hardly enamoured with Streisand, calling her "the most pretentious woman the cinema has ever known". But as the first woman to earn $5

ABOVE "Bogart and Hepburn give brilliant performances of such detail and subtlety," thought Clarissa Bowen in *Sight and Sound*. Katharine Hepburn as Rose and Humphrey Bogart as Charlie Allnutt in the successful *The African Queen*.

million for one film, *Nuts* (1987), she can probably learn to live with such insults.

Fewer female stars were being ranked in Quigley's top 10 by the seventies. Those that occasionally proved more popular than Streisand were usually just the latest flavour of the month. There was Ali McGraw, scoring a big success with *Love Story* (1970) and acting opposite future husband Steve McQueen in Sam Peckinpah's hit thriller *The Getaway* (1972). She's appeared in little of note since. Then there was child-actress Tatum O'Neal, who starred with her father Ryan in *Paper Moon* (1973) and won an Oscar for her performance. She had one more big hit with the routine *The Bad News Bears* (1976) before unsuccessfully attempting to graduate to adult roles. And finally Diane Keaton, who starred opposite her then real-life partner Woody Allen in a series of excellent comedies, proving particularly popular in *Annie Hall* (1977) and *Manhattan* (1979). Her neurotic roles were obviously partly based on herself. Woody Allen later claimed, "she has

no self-confidence. If there's a way to twist a compliment into an excuse for self-criticism, she'll find it."

The eighties produced no common trend; each year seemed to bring a new leading actress. At the turn of the decade it was Jane Fonda, who suddenly became a serious actress in the seventies following her marriage to Roger Vadim and the sci-fi sex comedy they made together, *Barbarella* (1967). In the late seventies Fonda starred in such worthy but slightly dull movies as Fred Zinnemann's *Julia* (1977), the nuclear warning thriller *The China Syndrome* (1979), the Vietnam veteran movie *Coming Home* (1978), the modern western with a message *The Electric Horseman* (1979) and the Colin Higgins comedy *Nine to Five* (1980), which hammered audiences with a feminist message and forgot to include the necessary funny jokes. The last also starred country singer Dolly Parton, who replaced Fonda as top box-office draw. Parton had another big hit with the musical *The Best Little Whorehouse in Texas* (1982), also starring the top male star

LEFT "I went from nothingness to political radicalness." Jane Fonda in the sci-fi sex comedy *Barbarella*, directed by her then husband Roger Vadim.

RIGHT *The French Lieutenant's Woman* director Karel Reisz felt that Meryl Streep "has a range of temperament that is very rare and a very special sort of daring". She certainly never got to display it in *Falling in Love,* an inferior rehash of *Brief Encounter* with Robert de Niro.

BELOW Fonda the serious actress, in the concerned nuclear-warning thriller *The China Syndrome.* Its release coincided with the similar Three Mile Island accident.

Burt Reynolds and again directed by Higgins. Thankfully lightning didn't strike twice when she teamed up with Stallone for *Rhinestone* (1984), although she was later in the popular *Steel Magnolias* (1989).

Meryl Streep seemed to earn an Oscar nomination for her every performance in the eighties, winning for *Kramer vs Kramer* (1979) and *Sophie's Choice* (1982), and twice found herself top female star, although the first time she was ranked only 12 overall. Streep's best role came when she broke away

★ NOTABLE FIRST ★

The first depiction of sexual intercourse in a mainstream movie occurred in the Czechoslovakian film *Extase* (1933), directed by former assistant to Erich Von Stroheim Gustav Machaty. The performers were Hedwig Kiesler and Aribert Mog. The actress later found fame in Hollywood after signing a contract with MGM and changing her name to Hedy Lamarr. However, for such a famed film, *Extase* was little seen. In America the film was ruled obscene and, despite the distributor's successful appeal, few cinemas were willing to book it, while Lamarr's millionaire husband, German munitions magnate Fritz Mandl, unhappy with his wife's public display, tried to purchase all available prints.

ABOVE Sally Field in the routine comedy *Surrender* (1987).

for the first time from her usual dignified middle-class parts – *Manhattan* (1979), *Falling in Love* (1984), *Plenty* (1985), *Heartburn* (1986) – and starred in the title role in *Silkwood* (1983), the true story of Karen Silkwood, who confronted the authorities over nuclear safety and later met a mysterious death. This was a more controversial role but was generally well received.

As TV star of *Gidget* and *The Flying Nun*, it is perhaps not surprising that ex-Tarzan Jock Mahoney's step-daughter, Sally Field, initially found "the material I was offered was terrible". She had her first taste of cinema success in a series of movies with Burt Reynolds. Field defended the likes of *Smokey and the Bandit* (1977) and *Hooper* (1978) by referring to them as "frivolous … mindless entertainment", claiming that "I

think that is valuable when it doesn't pretend to be anything else". She was obviously prouder of her later work, winning Oscars for Martin Ritt's union drama *Norma Rae* (1979) and the Depression-set *Places in the Heart* (1984), as well as starring with Paul Newman in *Absence of Malice* (1981) and James Garner in *Murphy's Romance* (1985). She disappeared from the screen for much of the late eighties, although was seen with fellow box-office stars Parton and Julia Roberts in *Steel Magnolias*.

Glenn Close emerged as a front-rank star in 1986, and was nominated for an Oscar for her supporting role in *The World According to Garp* (1982). She played noted parts in Lawrence Kasdan's ensemble piece *The Big Chill* (1983) and *The Natural* (1984) with Robert Redford. Close had a trio of hits, partner-

★ NOTABLE FIRSTS ★

The first all-dwarf cast appeared in *The Terror of Tiny Town* (1938), which was an otherwise straightforward western story of cattle rustling directed by the prolific Sam Newfeld. Newfeld also directed *Harlem on the Prairie* (1937), a rare all-black western, during the same period.

The largest all-female cast assembled for one film was 135 for MGM's *The Women* (1939), directed by George Cukor and featuring a host of female stars and up-and-coming actresses, including Joan Crawford, Norma Shearer, Rosalind Russell, Paulette Goddard and Joan Fontaine. The advertising played up the gimmick; "135 women with men on their minds!" claimed the posters. It was later remade as *The Opposite Sex* (1956).

ing Jeff Bridges in the well-received courtroom thriller *Jagged Edge* (1985), starring with Michael Douglas in the pretentious and sexist *Fatal Attraction* (1987) and opposite John Malkovich in Stephen Frears' *Dangerous Liaisons* (1988).

While Close is certainly a more interesting actress than Bette Midler, who has proved popular with routine comedies like *Down and Out in Beverly Hills* (1985), *Ruthless People* (1986) and *Big Business* (1988), she certainly pales in comparison to Kathleen Turner. Turner made an impressive debut, undoubtedly the best thing in Lawrence Kasdan's pseudo *film noir Body Heat* (1981). It brought comparisons with Lauren Bacall and Barbara Stanwyck, the latter the star of the very similar (and superior) *Double Indemnity* (1944). Her fame was sealed with the adventure comedy *Romancing the Stone* (1984) opposite Michael Douglas, with whom she later co-starred in an inferior sequel, *Jewel of the Nile* (1985), and the surprisingly bleak comedy *The War of the Roses* (1989). However, her best roles have been for her best directors: for John Huston in the mafia comedy *Prizzi's Honour* (1985), as the

RIGHT Glenn Close and John Malkovich in Stephen Frears' ***Dangerous Liaisons,*** **based on Christopher Hampton's play.**

prostitute China Blue in Ken Russell's much underrated *Crimes of Passion* (1984) and in Francis Coppola's marvellous tale of lost youth and innocence, *Peggy Sue Got Married* (1986).

Current top dog is Julia Roberts, sister of actor Eric Roberts. Her rise to the top has been meteoric, mainly through trite films like the prostitute-finds-true-love comedy *Pretty Woman* (1990), *Flatliners* (1990) and the incredibly slack thriller *Sleeping with the Enemy* (1991). Despite opening to dreadful reviews, *Sleeping with the Enemy* managed to gross over $100 million. Hollywood seems completely enamoured of Roberts, her *Flatliners* director Joel Schumacher's over-the-top comment that "she is unique, she is delicious, she is irresistible" being not untypical. But without some decent films, her fame may prove short-lived.

LEFT Julia Roberts in the vacuous *Sleeping with the Enemy*. Nevertheless, to date she has been Oscar nominated for her work in *Steel Magnolias* and *Pretty Woman*.

LEFT Perhaps not quite as good as her work with Coppola or Russell, Kathleen Turner was still excellent (opposite Jack Nicholson) in John Huston's *Prizzi's Honour*.

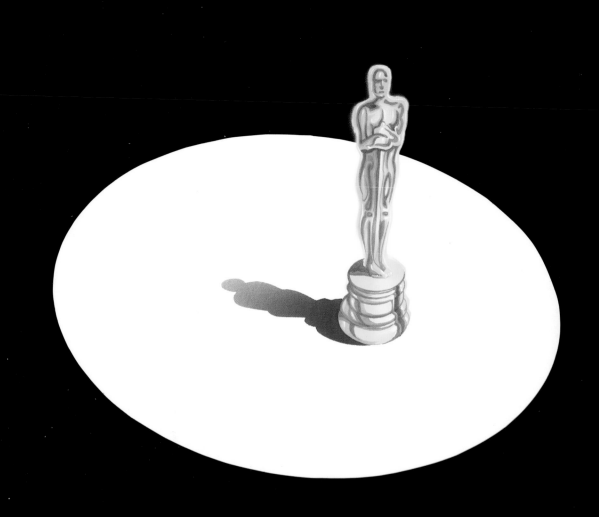

The Awards

THE SIGHT AND SOUND AWARDS

ight and Sound, the British Film Institute's prestigious film journal, has held a poll every 10 years since 1952 to determine the world's film critics' favourite movies. They are not asked to nominate the best – an impossible task – only their favourite 10, or, as the magazine put it, "the films that have been for them the most relevant, stimulating or enjoyable, their choices for a desert island or their first entries in a cassette collection". The first poll was intended to complement a similar exercise undertaken by the committee of the Festival Mondial du Film et des Beaux Arts de Belgique that same year. The major difference was that the Belgian survey was conducted mostly among film directors (directors were allowed to vote for their own movies; Cecil B DeMille nominated four of his), but surprisingly, there was a strong similarity between the two lists.

There have been four *Sight and Sound* polls, with only two films appearing every time; Sergei Eisenstein's *The Battleship Potemkin* and Jean Renoir's *La Règle du Jeu*, although *L'Avventura* and *8½* have featured in each poll since their release. In fact, in the last poll, held in 1982, *8½* was the newest film to appear. It was then nearly 20 years old. At least the latest poll revealed the widest number of titles, although the number of critics replying has grown from 63 to 122 over the 30 years.

In contrast with either the conservative character of current critics or their preference for older films, the first poll winner, *Bicycle Thieves*, had been released just four years earlier. *Bicycle Thieves* was the crowning achievement of Italian neo-realism, a style that made extensive use of real locations and non-actors in leading parts, creating a deglamorized documentary look to tell simple stories of working people. During the same period in British movies, the only working-class or regional accents heard were in small supporting

SIGHT AND SOUND 1952

		DIRECTOR	YEAR	VOTES
1	BICYCLE THIEVES	DE SICA	1948	25
2	CITY LIGHTS	CHAPLIN	1931	19
	THE GOLD RUSH	CHAPLIN	1925	19
4	THE BATTLESHIP POTEMKIN	EISENSTEIN	1925	16
5	LOUISIANA STORY	FLAHERTY	1948	12
	INTOLERANCE	GRIFFITH	1916	12
7	GREED	VON STROHEIM	1923	11
	LE JOUR SE LÈVE (DAYBREAK)	CARNE	1939	11
	THE PASSION OF JOAN OF ARC	DREYER	1928	11
10	BRIEF ENCOUNTER	LEAN	1945	10
	LE MILLION	CLAIR	1931	10
	LA RÈGLE DU JEU (THE RULES OF THE GAME)	RENOIR	1939	10

LEFT The famous Odessa steps scene from *The Battleship Potemkin*, recently aped to little effect by Brian de Palma in *The Untouchables*.

CINÉMATEQUE BELGIQUE 1952

		DIRECTOR	YEAR
1	THE BATTLESHIP POTEMKIN	EISENSTEIN	1925
2	THE GOLD RUSH	CHAPLIN	1925
3	BICYCLE THIEVES	DE SICA	1948
4	CITY LIGHTS	CHAPLIN	1931
	LA GRANDE ILLUSION	RENOIR	1937
	LE MILLION	CLAIR	1931
7	GREED	VON STROHEIM	1923
8	HALLELUJAH	VIDOR	1929
9	DIE DREIGROSCHENOPER (THE THREEPENNY OPERA)	PABST	1931
	BRIEF ENCOUNTER	LEAN	1945
	INTOLERANCE	GRIFFITH	1916
	MAN OF ARAN	FLAHERTY	1934

SIGHT AND SOUND 1962

		DIRECTOR	YEAR	VOTES
1	CITIZEN KANE	WELLES	1941	22
2	L'AVVENTURA	ANTONIONI	1960	20
3	LA RÈGLE DU JEU	RENOIR	1939	19
4	GREED	VON STROHEIM	1923	17
	UGETSU MONOGATARI	MIZOGUCHI	1953	17
7	THE BATTLESHIP POTEMKIN	EISENSTEIN	1925	16
	BICYCLE THIEVES	DE SICA	1948	16
	IVAN THE TERRIBLE	EISENSTEIN	1942-6	16
9	LA TERRA TREMA	VISCONTI	1948	14
10	L'ATALANTE	VIGO	1934	13

RIGHT Nora Gregor and director Jean Renoir during the making of *La Règle du Jeu*.

roles, with the exception of comedy stars like George Formby and Gracie Fields. Little wonder the scholarly critics were so enthusiastic. Neo-realism's impact was seen even in Hollywood, particularly in the location-shot thrillers like *The Naked City* (1948). *The Naked City*'s narrator's comment – "There are eight million stories in the naked city. This has been one of them" – would have been supported by the neo-realists.

Bicycle Thieves was made by the director-writer team of Vittorio de Sica and Cesare Zavattini, who had first worked together in 1942 on *The Children Are Watching Us*. The story is simple. Antonio (Lamberto Maggiorani) has been unemployed for two years when he is offered a job as a bill-poster, on the condition he has a bike. His wife, Maria (Lianella Carell), retrieves Antonio's bicycle from the pawnshop, but it is stolen on his first day. The police are unsympathetic, and so the following day is spent searching the streets of Rome, with only his son Bruno (Enzo Staiola) for company. It is a heart-

breaking film, from Alessandro Cicognini's haunting music to the beaten, desolate face of Antonio at the finale, jostled by the large football crowd and in tears at the humiliation of having been caught stealing a bike after failing to find his own, holding on to his small son's hand. The only relief is in the caring relationships between Antonio and Bruno and, to a lesser extent, Antonio and Maria. The father-son relationship is unobtrusively yet constantly present – Bruno always looking up at his father, walking close to his side and the manner in which he imitates his father as Antonio gets ready for work. Best of all is the scene where Antonio slaps Bruno out of frustration, which is followed a little later by Antonio's panic on hearing the shouts of "he's drowning", fearing it might be Bruno. Their looks of reproach and regret are perfect.

Equally impressive are the war-torn locations and the pervading sense of poverty created by de Sica, particularly in the pawnshop scene: there's the distinguished-looking gentleman

BICYCLE THIEVES

THE NOVEL OF THE FAMOUS PRIZE-WINNING ITALIAN FILM – POSTWAR ROME AND THE WARPED SOULS OF ITS UNDERWORLD

Initially Welles was to have directed and starred in an adaptation of Joseph Conrad's *Heart of Darkness*, written by Welles with John Houseman, but the budget proved too great. However, Welles didn't waste his time. He studied scores of films to learn the tricks of the trade, particularly from John Ford. He later said: "John Ford was my teacher. My own style has nothing to do with his, but *Stagecoach* (1939) was my movie textbook. I ran it over 40 times."

So Welles turned to a project called *American*, later re-named *John Citizen USA* and finally *Citizen Kane* The script was worked on by Herman J Mankiewicz, then heavily revised by Welles. Welles' contribution to the script became the centre of Pauline Kael's controversial article in *The New Yorker*, in which she claimed the work was mostly Mankiewicz's. But as John Houseman, who worked with Mankiewicz on the

LEFT During the production of *Bicycle Thieves* 22 per cent of the Italian workforce was unemployed.

BELOW "Marvellously exciting, stimulating, maddening, frustrating" was editor Robert Wise's verdict on working with Orson Welles on *Citizen Kane*, seen here directing *The Lady from Shanghai* (1948).

trying to pawn his binoculars, and the endless stacks of pawned sheets and clothes. This is nicely contrasted with the glamour of Hollywood, with Antonio shown putting up Rita Hayworth posters.

Vittorio de Sica was a director much admired by the great Orson Welles, particularly for his earlier *Shoeshine* (1946). "What de Sica can do, I can't do. I ran over *Shoeshine* recently and the camera disappeared, the screen disappeared, it was just like life." It was Welles' first film, *Citizen Kane*, which replaced *Bicycle Thieves* at the top of the next *Sight and Sound* poll, a position it has since maintained.

When Welles arrived in Hollywood in 1939 at the age of 24 he was already nationally famous, especially for his radio production of H G Wells' *The War of the Worlds*. It was presented as a news bulletin and caused nationwide panic. His critical reputation was also assured by the Mercury Theater's audacious productions of *Julius Caesar* and *Macbeth*, the latter with an all-black cast. The combination resulted in a *carte blanche* contract for Welles from RKO. He would receive $150,000 per picture plus 25 per cent of gross receipts, was free to work as director, writer, producer, star or any combination of the four, and had total artistic control. RKO's only power was financial. As Welles later remarked, "I started at the top and worked down". Not surprisingly, such unprecedented treatment created much resentment in Hollywood.

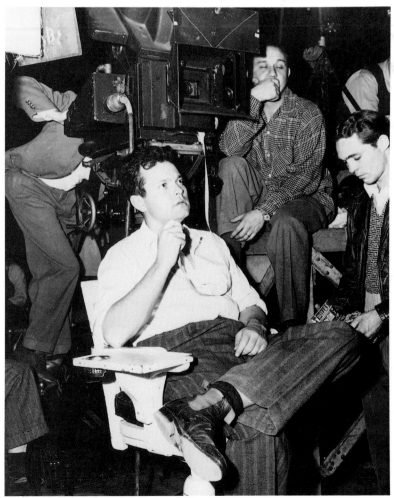

SIGHT AND SOUND 1972

	DIRECTOR	YEAR	VOTES
1 CITIZEN KANE	WELLES	1941	32
2 LA RÈGLE DU JEU	RENOIR	1939	28
3 THE BATTLESHIP POTEMKIN	EISENSTEIN	1925	16
4 8½	FELLINI	1963	15
5 L'AVVENTURA	ANTONIONI	1960	12
PERSONA	BERGMAN	1966	12
7 THE PASSION OF JOAN OF ARC	DREYER	1928	11
8 THE GENERAL	KEATON/BRUCKMAN	1926	10
THE MAGNIFICENT AMBERSONS	WELLES	1942	10
10 UGETSU MONOGATARI	MIZOGUCHI	1953	9
WILD STRAWBERRIES	BERGMAN	1957	9

SIGHT AND SOUND 1982

	DIRECTOR	YEAR	VOTES
1 CITIZEN KANE	WELLES	1941	45
2 LA RÈGLE DU JEU	RENOIR	1939	31
3 SEVEN SAMURAI	KUROSAWA	1954	15
4 SINGIN' IN THE RAIN	DONEN/KELLY	1952	15
5 8½	FELLINI	1963	14
6 THE BATTLESHIP POTEMKIN	EISENSTEIN	1925	13
7 L'AVVENTURA	ANTONIONI	1960	12
THE MAGNIFICENT AMBERSONS	WELLES	1942	12
VERTIGO	HITCHCOCK	1958	12
10 THE GENERAL	KEATON/BRUCKMAN	1926	11
THE SEARCHERS	FORD	1956	11

script, stated: "He [Welles] added a great deal of material himself, and later he and Herman had a dreadful row over the screen credit. As far as I could judge, the co-billing was correct. The *Citizen Kane* script was the product of both of them."

The influence of Gregg Toland, the film's cinematographer, has never been doubted. It was Toland who approached Welles, believing that if Welles was "left alone as much as possible we're going to have a picture that looks different". Fortunately they did. The oft-mentioned effects – the use of ceilings, the deep focus, expressionistic lighting and overlapping dialogue – were not seen for the first time; but never before had they been used together to such effect. Welles readily acknowledged Toland's contribution with a prominent title credit, rare for a cinematographer in 1941. Mention should also be made of the Mercury Theater performers, such as Joseph Cotten in the role of Leland, Agnes Moorehead as Kane's mother and Everett Sloane as Bernstein, making their film debuts, as was Welles, giving a magnificent performance in the title role, ageing from 25 to 70.

Citizen Kane, as is well known, was heavily influenced by the life of newspaper tycoon William Randolph Hearst. But it is not a straightforward telling of the story. It opens on a "No Trespassing" sign, continues with images of a decaying

LEFT "He never believed in anything except Charlie Kane." Kane as aspiring politician.

ABOVE "I think it would be fun to run a newspaper." Kane as press baron, with Leland (Cotten).

mansion, shows a glass ball dropping to the floor and a close-up of a man's lips whispering "Rosebud", followed by a nurse reflected in the same glass ball: not a conventional opening sequence. The film continues to play with the narrative and audience expectations. A newsreel chronicles the life of Charles Foster Kane, followed by a scene in a screening-room where the newsreel is criticized. The audience feel like eavesdroppers, as the characters' faces remain mostly in shadow. Welles even avoids providing a clear look at Thompson, the reporter sent on the quest to discover the meaning of Kane's last word – "Rosebud".

The film follows Thompson as he visits the Thatcher Memorial Library, Kane's ex-wife Susan Alexander, his ex-general manager Bernstein and college friend Leland, learn-

ing about Kane's days running the *New York Inquirer*, his failed bid to enter politics and his two marriages. Thompson ends up at Kane's mansion Xanadu, talking to Kane's cold and dispassionate butler. The meaning of "Rosebud" eludes Thompson, but not the audience; it was the name of the sledge Kane had owned as a child when he was taken from his parents by Mr Thatcher. However, as Thompson comes to realize, Rosebud "wouldn't have explained anything. Rosebud is just a piece of a jigsaw puzzle." It is a MacGuffin – a device important to the characters but not especially to the audience – to rival anything used by Hitchcock. However, director Martin Scorsese considers "Rosebud" works on a more substantial level than a mere MacGuffin. "The beauty of the 'Rosebud' idea that stays with you is the lost innocence,

★ NOTABLE FIRST ★

The first three-colour Technicolor feature was Rouben Mamoulian's *Becky Sharp* (1935), produced by RKO and starring Miriam Hopkins in the title role, Cedric Hardwicke, Alan Mowbray and Frances Dee. RKO selected its material well. A period drama was perfect for displaying the virtues of colour and *Becky Sharp* was based on Langden Mitchell's stage adaptation of Thackeray's *Vanity Fair*. Mamoulian was an equally wise choice, having a reputation as a stylish director willing to experiment.

the melancholy of the inspiration that you had when you were young, and how it changes, how it survives, and doesn't survive, in your own estimation. That initial spark that you want to hold on to until the end of your life, and how it eludes some people, and how it seemed to elude him."

Throughout *Kane* we are treated to some memorable dialogue: Kane's assertion that "If I hadn't been very rich I might have been a very great man"; an old Bernstein claiming that old age "is the only disease you don't look forward to being cured of"; Kane's introduction to Susan Alexander, "I run a couple of newspapers. What do you do?"; Leland's comment on Kane building Xanadu, "He was disappointed with the world, so he built one of his own"; and, best of all, Bernstein talking about a girl he saw one day in 1896, "I only saw her

for a second. She didn't see me at all. But I bet a month hasn't gone by since that I haven't thought about that girl." There are an equal number of great scenes, too many to list, although the celebrated breakfast scenes economically illustrating Kane's dying marriage to Emily, and Kane's childish, violent destruction of Susan's room after she leaves him stand out in particular.

Kane's subject caused a storm of controversy on release. Louis B Mayer offered RKO the $450,000 negative costs to destroy the picture, and the Hearst newspapers, led by gossip columnist Louella Parsons, ran a vicious campaign against Welles – for example accusing him of being a Communist and questioning why he had not been drafted. The Radio City Music Hall, where *Kane* was originally to have opened on 14

ABOVE "You never give me anything I really care about." Kane (Welles) and second wife Susan Alexander (Dorothy Cumingore).

February 1941, refused to show the film. For his part, Welles threatened to sue RKO if they did not release his picture. The film finally opened on 1 May 1941 to uniformly excellent reviews. It received nine Oscar nominations, although only its screenplay won. It was voted second behind Preston Sturges' *The Lady Eve* (1941) on the *New York Times* annual "Ten Best" list and was named Best Film in the New York Film Critics awards and the National Board of Review awards.

But the Hearst campaign hurt the picture and *Citizen Kane* was not a financial success. The big cinema circuits refused to screen the picture and it lost $150,000 on initial release. Reportedly, Hearst wasn't actually angered by the film, but it was his mistress, actress Marion Davies, and the comparisons with the Susan Alexander character that caused most offence. Susan Alexander is presented as an inept opera singer, forced into her career by Kane, and Welles concurs that "we were very unfair to Marion Davies . . . it seems to me something of a dirty trick". Welles also told of the extent to which Hearst went to exact revenge: "I was lecturing in Buffalo. After the

lecture I was having dinner with some people and the waiter said there's a policeman wants to see you. I turned white, I always feel guilty when policemen want to see me. The cop turned out to be very nice. He said, 'Don't go back to your hotel room.' I said, 'Why?', and he said, 'They've got an underage girl, undressed, and photographers waiting for you. It's a set up'."

The problems with *Kane* might have resulted in the infamous 1942 trade ad that proclaimed "Showmanship in place of genius: a new deal at RKO", but *Kane*'s reputation continues to grow. In 1982 *Sight and Sound* felt that "in 1992, if there should be another round of the game, we won't be at all surprised if the verdict is still *Citizen Kane* first, the rest nowhere". They are probably right. In 1989, when the British magazine *Time Out* conducted a similar poll among 60 film directors and critics, *Citizen Kane* came out on top again.

Kane's impact has been immense. Scorsese describes it thus: "*Citizen Kane* was a picture that made you think anything was possible on film, and that's important. I think the sense of ambition in the film was very strong, the sense of wanting to be everything a film could be, stretching the limits of film. I think that's what's always inspiring about it."

ABOVE An original sketch for the final scene set at Xanadu in *Citizen Kane*.

TIME OUT POLL 1989

		DIRECTOR	YEAR
1	CITIZEN KANE	WELLES	1941
2	THE THIRD MAN	REED	1949
3	THE NIGHT OF THE HUNTER	LAUGHTON	1955
4	SOME LIKE IT HOT	WILDER	1959
5	THE GODFATHER	COPPOLA	1972
6	VERTIGO	HITCHCOCK	1958
7	L'ATALANTE	VIGO	1934
8	RAGING BULL	SCORSESE	1980
9	LES ENFANTS DU PARADIS	CARNÉ	1945
10	NORTH BY NORTHWEST	HITCHCOCK	1959

THE OSCARS

The Academy Awards ceremony was first held on 16 May 1929, organized by the recently formed Academy of Motion Picture Arts and Sciences to raise the "cultural, educational and scientific standards" of the industry. It was hoped to improve Hollywood's reputation following the scandals of the twenties, hence its rather sombre and dignified name.

THE FILMS

The first Best Picture winner was former pilot William Wellman's First World War flying movie *Wings* (1927), starring Clara Bow, Richard Arlen and Charles "Buddy" Rogers and featuring some fine aerial sequences. *Wings* was also a huge hit, taking $3.8 million at the box-office. Not surprisingly, given that *The Jazz Singer* (1927) had already introduced dialogue to the feature film, *Wings* remains the only non-talkie to win the Best Picture Oscar.

However, *Wings* won only one other Oscar, for Best Engineering Effects. This pales compared with *Ben Hur* (1959; see below), which took a record 11 Oscars. Following close behind are Robert Wise's *Romeo and Juliet*-inspired musical *West Side Story* (1961), starring Natalie Wood and Richard Beymer, and *Gone with the Wind* (1939), each with 10 Oscars to their credit.

RIGHT Charles Rogers (left) and Richard Arlen (right) in *Wings*. The Academy's first Best Picture was also named on *The New York Times* "Ten Best" list for 1927.

LEFT Charlton Heston, Sam Jaffe, Martha Scott, Haya Harareet and Cathy O'Donnell in William Wyler's record Oscar winner, *Ben Hur*.

None of the above films received as many nominations as *All About Eve* (1950), which, with a grand total of 14, became the most nominated film. Joseph L Mankiewicz's drama of New York theatre life won a respectable six statuettes, including one for George Sanders as Best Supporting Actor, the coveted Best Picture award and two for Mankiewicz, as both director and scriptwriter. Amazingly, Judy Holliday's dumb blonde Billie Dawn in *Born Yesterday* (1950) was preferred to Bette Davis' performance as ageing star Margo Channing. The Cannes Film Festival and New York Film Critics both made amends by presenting Davis with their awards for Best Actress.

At least *All About Eve* received six of its 14 possible awards and didn't suffer the ignominy of being labelled the most nominated film not to win an Oscar. That honour is shared by Herbert Ross' dull ballet drama *The Turning Point* (1977), starring Oscar-nominated trio Anne Bancroft, Shirley MacLaine and Mikhail Baryshinkov, and Steven Spielberg's *The Color Purple* (1985), the story of life among the black community in the American South during the first half of the 20th century. Both movies received 11 nominations.

BEN HUR (11 OSCARS)

BEST PICTURE	
BEST DIRECTION	SAM ZIMBALIST (PRODUCER)
BEST ACTOR	WILLIAM WYLER
BEST SUPPORTING ACTOR	CHARLTON HESTON
BEST COLOUR CINEMATOGRAPHY	HUGH GRIFFITH
BEST ART (SET) DIRECTION	ROBERT SURTEES
	WILLIAM A HORNING,
BEST COLOUR COSTUME DESIGN	EDWARD CARFAGNO, HUGH HUNT
BEST EDITING	ELIZABETH HAFFENDEN
BEST SOUND	RALPH E WINTERS, JOHN D DUNNING
BEST SPECIAL EFFECTS	FRANKLIN E MILTON
	A ARNOLD GILLESPIE, ROBERT
BEST MUSIC SCORE OF A COMEDY OR DRAMA	MACDONALD, MILO LEVY
	MIKLOS ROZSA

RIGHT Frank Capra's wonderful romantic comedy, *It Happened One Night*, the first winner of all five major Oscars.

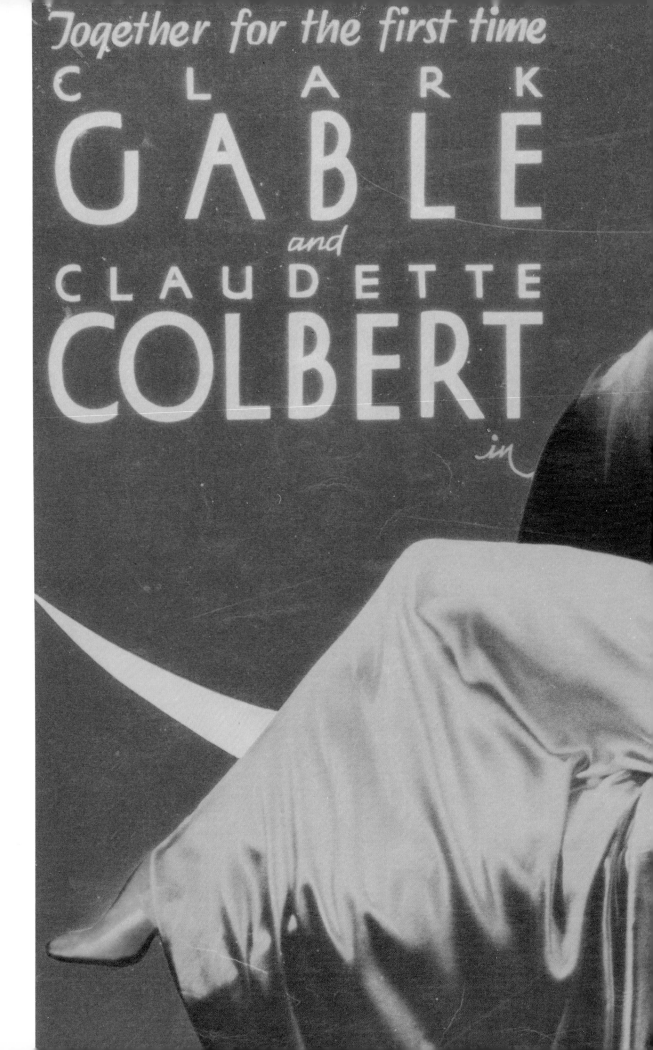

Together for the first time

CLARK

GABLE

and

CLAUDETTE

COLBERT

in

"It Happened One Night"

with WALTER CONNOLLY · ROSCOE KARNS

From the Cosmopolitan Magazine story by SAMUEL HOPKINS ADAMS

Screen play by ROBERT RISKIN

FRANK CAPRA Production

The Informer was also notable for producing the first Oscar refusal, when Dudley Nichols turned down his award because of a union boycott of the ceremony. Ford collected his next Oscars at the beginning of the forties, winning in successive years for the classic Depression drama *The Grapes of Wrath* (1940), based on the John Steinbeck novel, and *How Green Was My Valley* (1941), a highly Hollywoodized notion of life in a Welsh mining village. The only other director to equal this feat is Joseph L Mankiewicz, who almost 10 years later won in consecutive years for *Letter to Three Wives* (1949) and *All About Eve* (1950). Ford's last Oscar triumph came with the John Wayne Irish comedy *The Quiet Man* (1952). He was thus neglected for his most famous works, marvellous westerns like *Stagecoach* (1939), *My Darling Clementine* (1946), *The Searchers* (1956) and *The Man Who Shot Liberty Valance* (1962). But then the western has only just fared slightly better than the horror film at Oscar time.

ABOVE *The Color Purple*, like many Spielberg movies, was overlooked on Oscar night.

Finally, only two films have won the five major Oscars: Best Picture, Director, Actor, Actress and Screenplay. Unexpectedly, both were deserving cases. The first to achieve the feat was Frank Capra's captivating romantic comedy *It Happened One Night* (1934), in which runaway heiress Claudette Colbert and newspaper reporter Clark Gable fall in love on a cross-country bus journey. Columbia boss Harry Cohn, Capra, Gable, Colbert and scriptwriter Robert Riskin were the Oscar winners. The film was also an unexpected box-office winner, having been released with little ballyhoo and to generally lukewarm reviews. It took 31 years for another film to repeat the achievement. In 1975 Milos Forman's *One Flew Over the Cuckoo's Nest* (1975) swept the awards, featuring a powerful performance from Jack Nicholson as the drifter who feigns mental illness to avoid prison and then attempts to enliven the inmates of a mental ward. Louise Fletcher as Nurse Ratchet, Lawrence Hauben and Bo Goldman's script and Michael Douglas and Saul Zaentz's production were the other winners.

THE DIRECTORS

RIGHT The great John Ford, recipient of four Best Director Oscars.

The man with the most Best Director Oscars is John Ford, whose four awards edge out Frank Capra and William Wyler (who has a record 12 nominations), who have three apiece. Ford's triumphs came over a 17-year period, starting with *The Informer* in 1935, a tale of betrayal during the Irish rebellion.

THE ACTORS

Five actors have two Best Actor Oscars to their name. The first double winner was Spencer Tracy, who is also the only star to have won the award in consecutive years. His performances as the fisherman in an adaptation of Rudyard Kipling's *Captains Courageous* (1937) and as Father Flanagan in the sentimental box-office hit *Boys' Town* (1938) brought him his two Oscars. Fredric March became the second double Oscar winner in 1946 after starring in William Wyler's *The Best Years of Our Lives* (1946) see page 20). He had won his first Oscar 14 years earlier for *Dr Jekyll and Mr Hyde* (1931), which is both the only time an actor has been honoured for a horror movie and the only time there has been a tie for the award. March's first moment of triumph was shared by Wallace Beery for his part in the tear-jerking boxing drama *The Champ* (1931).

The next to join the exclusive club was Gary Cooper, for playing the title-role of First World War hero *Sergeant York* (1941) and starring in Fred Zinnemann's seminal western *High Noon* (1952). Two years later Marlon Brando won the first of his Oscars, giving his "I could have been a contender" speech in Elia Kazan's union drama *On the Waterfront* (1954). Brando's second success came as Don Vito Corleone in *The Godfather* (1972). On this occasion he sent an actress posing as American Indian, Sacheen Littlefeather, to collect his award, in protest at the treatment the Indians have received in film and television. The most recent star to become a double Oscar winner is Dustin Hoffman, successful in *Kramer vs Kramer* (1979), which considered Hoffman being able to look after his own son almost worthy of sainthood, and as an autistic in the equally self-important *Rain Man* (1988).

The most nominated best actors are Spencer Tracy and Laurence Olivier, who both won nine nominations over the

LEFT Gary Cooper (third right) and Grace Kelly (far right) in *High Noon*. Cooper is best known for his roles in westerns.

years. Olivier collected his only Oscar in 1948 for his performance in the title role of *Hamlet* (1948), a film he also directed. The most unfortunate actors must be Richard Burton and Peter O'Toole, nominated on seven occasions but never winners. But then Burton wasn't even nominated for probably his best performance, as angry young man Jimmy Porter in *Look Back in Anger* (1959).

RIGHT Spencer Tracy won his second Oscar as Father Flanagan in *Boys' Town*, seen here with leading box-office star Mickey Rooney.

RIGHT Dustin Hoffman gave his first Oscar-winning performance in *Kramer vs Kramer*, seen with eight-year-old Justin Henry who became the youngest star to be nominated for a regular Oscar.

SPENCER TRACY'S OSCAR NOMINATIONS

1936	SAN FRANCISCO
1937	CAPTAINS COURAGEOUS
1938	BOYS' TOWN
1950	FATHER OF THE BRIDE
1955	BAD DAY AT BLACK ROCK
1958	THE OLD MAN AND THE SEA
1960	INHERIT THE WIND
1961	JUDGEMENT AT NUREMBURG
1967	GUESS WHO'S COMING TO DINNER?

LAURENCE OLIVIER'S OSCAR NOMINATIONS

1939	WUTHERING HEIGHTS
1940	REBECCA
1946	HENRY V
1948	HAMLET
1956	RICHARD III
1965	OTHELLO
1972	SLEUTH
1978	THE BOYS FROM BRAZIL

LEFT Laurence Olivier, nominated Best Actor for four Shakespeare roles, seen here in *Richard III*.

The first narrative film is often erroneously considered to be ex-Edison employee Edwin S Porter's self-explanatory western *The Great Train Robbery* (1903). However, the Lumières had made comic shorts like *L'Arrosseur Arrossé* as early as 1897, French film-maker George Méliès had been making popular fantasies like *A Trip to the Moon* (1902) and even Porter had made *The Life of an American Fireman* (1902) a year earlier, to name but a few previous examples. Nevertheless, Porter's 10-minute western was both very popular and highly influential.

LEFT Richard Burton and Peter O'Toole, seen together in *Becket*, share the unwanted record of the most nominated actors never to have won an Oscar. They were both beaten for *Becket* by Rex Harrison's performance in *My Fair Lady* (1964).

PETER O'TOOLE'S OSCAR NOMINATIONS

1962	LAWRENCE OF ARABIA
1964	BECKET
1968	THE LION IN WINTER
1969	GOODBYE MR CHIPS
1972	THE RULING CLASS
1980	THE STUNT MAN
1982	MY FAVOURITE YEAR

RICHARD BURTON'S OSCAR NOMINATIONS

1952	MY COUSIN RACHEL
1953	THE ROBE
1964	BECKET
1965	THE SPY WHO CAME IN FROM THE COLD
1966	WHO'S AFRAID OF VIRGINIA WOOLF?
1969	ANNE OF THE THOUSAND DAYS
1977	EQUUS

THE ACTRESSES

By contrast, one actress dominates the Best Actress records: Katharine Hepburn has won a record-breaking four Best Actress Oscars and received a total of 12 nominations. She first won in the year following her movie debut, for her performance in the backstage theatre drama *Morning Glory* (1933). She was ably supported by Adolphe Menjou and Douglas Fairbanks Jnr, although it is not quite the equal of her later film about struggling actresses, *Stage Door* (1937), where she was again supported by Menjou. Hepburn had to wait 34 years for her next Oscar, which came for Stanley Kramer's patronizing drama of racial intolerance, *Guess Who's Coming to Dinner?* (1967). It co-starred Spencer Tracy in his last role, and Hepburn claimed that her Oscar was really meant for them both.

Hepburn's next Oscar followed a year later when she starred with Peter O'Toole in *The Lion in Winter* (1968). It was both the only occasion the Best Actress Oscar was shared, Barbra Streisand also being honoured for her performance in *Funny Girl* (1968), and only the second time an actress had won in consecutive years. The first was Luise Rainer, for *The Great Ziegfeld* (1936) and *The Good Earth* (1937) Hepburn's last Oscar to date was awarded for the sentimental *On Golden Pond* (1981). The film also won an Oscar for Henry Fonda in his last feature film.

One record not held by Hepburn is the most consecutive nominations. That is shared by Bette Davis and Greer Garson,

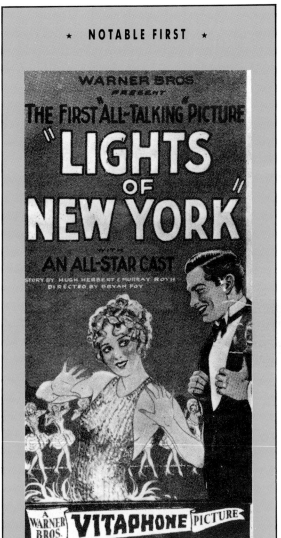

★ NOTABLE FIRST ★

WARNER BROS PRESENT
THE FIRST ALL-TALKING PICTURE
"LIGHTS OF NEW YORK"
WITH AN ALL-STAR CAST
STORY BY HUGH HERBERT & MURRAY ROTH
DIRECTED BY BRYAN FOY

A WARNER BROS. VITAPHONE PICTURE

The first all-talking picture was produced by Warner Brothers, the 57-minute *Lights of New York* (1928) starring Helene Costello, which was premiered in New York on 6 July 1928. The director, Bryan Foy, made his feature film debut but, having worked on numerous Vitaphone musical shorts, was at least no stranger to sound. The film was panned by the critics but was a hit nevertheless, the $75,000 investment returning $2 million at the box-office.

KATHARINE HEPBURN'S OSCAR NOMINATIONS

1933	MORNING GLORY
1935	ALICE ADAMS
1940	THE PHILADELPHIA STORY
1942	WOMAN OF THE YEAR
1951	THE AFRICAN QUEEN
1955	SUMMERTIME
1956	THE RAINMAKER
1959	SUDDENLY LAST SUMMER
1962	LONG DAY'S JOURNEY INTO NIGHT
1967	GUESS WHO'S COMING TO DINNER?
1968	THE LION IN WINTER
1981	ON GOLDEN POND

BETTE DAVIS' FIVE CONSECUTIVE OSCAR NOMINATIONS

1938	JEZEBEL
1939	DARK VICTORY
1940	THE LETTER
1941	THE LITTLE FOXES
1942	NOW VOYAGER

GREER GARSON'S FIVE CONSECUTIVE OSCAR NOMINATIONS

1941	BLOSSOMS IN THE DUST
1942	MRS MINIVER
1943	MADAME CURIE
1944	MRS SKEFFINGTON
1945	THE VALLEY OF DECISION

DEBORAH KERR'S OSCAR NOMINATIONS

1949	EDWARD, MY SON
1953	FROM HERE TO ETERNITY
1956	THE KING AND I
1957	HEAVEN KNOWS, MR ALLISON
1958	SEPARATE TABLES
1960	THE SUNDOWNERS

who chalked up five each. Both won once, Davis for the Civil War melodrama *Jezebel* (1938) and Garson for the much-loved Second World War morale booster *Mrs Miniver* (1942). The actress with the most nominations not to have won is the unfortunate Deborah Kerr. Perhaps this is because she wasn't even nominated for some of her best films, like the British movies *The Life and Death of Colonel Blimp* (1943), *Black Narcissus* (1947) and *The Innocents* (1961).

THE GOLDEN TURKEY AWARDS

In their 1978 publication, *The Fifty Worst Films of All Time*, the Medved brothers asked their readers to vote for the Worst Film of All Time, resulting in their influential book *The Golden Turkey Awards*. This, in turn, led to a dramatic increase of interest in "bad" movies. It's a pity that the Medveds at times display a condescending attitude to both their audience and their material. The majority of the films may have been bad, but at least Ed Wood, Phil Tucker *et al* made films. It was also never properly questioned as to what should qualify as a bad film.

The film topping the list is Ed D Wood Jnr's *Plan 9 from Outer Space*. It may be frequently inept, but it is always enter-taining and still revived in cinemas around the world, while many of its dull contemporaries are forgotten. Surely the Worst Film of All Time shouldn't be entertaining! Perhaps more deserving are the films of Jean-Luc Godard or Andy Warhol, or overblown epics like *The Greatest Story Ever Told* (1965). There are even more deserving films among low-budget B-movies and exploitation flicks; anything by Andy Milligan, who was the talent behind *The Rats Are Coming! The Werewolves Are Here!* (1972), or Al Adamson, director of the subtly titled *Brain of Blood* (1971), among others. But the popularity of the Medveds' book has saddled *Plan 9 From Outer Space* with the title the Worst Film of All Time.

RIGHT *Plan 9 from Outer Space* is regarded as the Worst Film of All Time; the result of bad sequence changes, inept acting and laughable dialogue.

THE GOLDEN TURKEY AWARDS

		DIRECTOR	YEAR	VOTES
1	PLAN 9 FROM OUTER SPACE (GRAVE ROBBERS FROM OUTER SPACE)	WOOD JNR	1959	393
2	EXORCIST II: THE HERETIC	BOORMAN	1977	384
3	KING KONG	GUILLERMIN	1976	283
4	THE SWARM	ALLEN	1978	249
5	SERGEANT PEPPER'S LONELY HEARTS CLUB BAND	SCHULTZ	1978	233
6	AIRPORT '77	JAMESON	1977	219
7	ORCA – KILLER WHALE	ANDERSON	1977	217
8	AIRPORT 1975	SMIGHT	1974	209
9	AT LONG LAST LOVE	BOGDANOVICH	1975	186
10	GREASE	KLEISER	1978	167

BELOW John Boorman's critically panned *Exorcist II: The Heretic.*

ABOVE Vampira as the old man's wife who died, and was then resurrected in *Plan 9 from Outer Space.*

That is not to say that *Plan 9* is well made. Sequences change from night to day, cardboard gravestones wobble, the burning flying saucers at the film's conclusion were paper plates on fire, the sets are (at best) minimal, the acting is frequently inept (a favourite being the cop scratching his neck with his gun barrel) and the dialogue often risible. Take

the opening, when the magnificent Criswell (fifties television personality, star of *Criswell Predicts*) informs the audience: "Greetings my friends. We are all interested in the future for that is where you and I are going to spend the rest of our lives. And remember my friends, future events such as these will effect you in the future . . ." And so on, all written by Criswell himself.

In fact, the film is full of choice dialogue. Criswell again, in a wonderfully pompous narration, describes the sorrow felt by the old man after his wife's death: "The sky where she had once looked was now only a covering for her dead body." "The ever-beautiful flowers she had planted with her own hands became nothing more than the lost roses of her cheeks." Criswell doesn't have a monopoly on dumb lines. On hearing of the flying saucer her husband has just seen, Paula Trent asks "A flying saucer? You mean the kind from up there?"; or there's the cop who observes, "Inspector Clay's dead. Murdered! And somebody's responsible!"

The film tells of two aliens, Eros and Tanna, who are ordered to stop the Earthlings from developing the solaronite

LEFT Dudley Manlove and Joanna Lee as the two aliens, Eros and Tanna, in *Plan 9 from Outer Space.*

bomb by the Ruler and decide to put into operation plan nine: resurrecting the recent dead. Although they seem pleased with the results, they are not terribly successful. Only three corpses are revived; the old man (played by Bela Lugosi for two minutes, but then doubled by Woods' chiropractor, a foot taller than Lugosi and bearing little physical resemblance), the old man's wife (Vampira, a fifties television horror host) and Inspector Clay (400lb Swedish wrestler Tor Johnson).

The life of Ed Wood has also attracted plenty of attention, and it is indeed as interesting as his films. He was a transvestite who claimed to have landed on a Pacific island during the war wearing pink bra and knickers under his uniform. His first film was, in fact, about transvestitism, *Glen or Glenda?* (1953; *I Changed My Sex, He or She?* and *I Led Two Lives*), a movie to rival *Plan 9*. *Glen or Glenda?* interweaves Glen's dilemma over whether to reveal his transvestitism to his fiancé Barbara, Bela Lugosi making absurd pronouncements from his armchair about "big green dragons that sit on your doorstep and eat little boys", and a ridiculous amount of stock footage.

> ★ **NOTABLE FIRST** ★
>
> *The only film in Smell-O-Vision* was Michael Todd Jnr's Canadian thriller *Scent of Mystery* (1959), which starred Denholm Elliott and Peter Lorre. This routine movie's fame is entirely based on it being the first "smellie", with specific scents released into the cinema at the required moment. John Waters also attempted a "smellie", providing audiences scratch and sniff cards for *Polyster* (1981), starring Divine. The odours this time were less pleasant.

We were also treated to Wood's fetishism for angora sweaters for the first time, later to reappear in his script for *The Bride and the Beast* (1958). According to Valda Hansen, who appeared in Wood's *Night of the Ghouls* (1959), "He had an angora dress, a pink one, that he was gorgeous in with his green eyes".

Despite the incredibly low budgets of his films, in the sixties Wood found it difficult to raise finance and turned to writing sex novels, with titles like *Killer in Drag, 69 Rue Pigalle* and *Diary of a Transvestite Hooker*, sometimes under the pseudonym Angora Peters. One was turned into a movie, *Orgy of the Dead* (1965), made from a script by Wood. He died, almost penniless, aged 54 in 1978, just before his films started receiving attention. According to his ex-wife Dolores Fuller (Barbara in *Glen or Glenda?*), "He'd be very pleased that some sort of acclaim has been given to him".

Plan 9 From Outer Space was the only movie in the Golden Turkey top 10 to be released before 1974, which only proves that most movie-goers have short memories. When bad film festivals came into fashion, it wasn't the recent releases that were dragged out, but grade Z productions from the fifties and sixties. So what qualities did these films need?

Some films' reputations rest entirely on having absurd titles, like William Beaudine's double bill of *Billy the Kid Versus Dracula* (1965) and *Jesse James Meets Frankenstein's Daughter* (1965; although it's actually his granddaughter) or Ray Dennis Steckler's *The Incredibly Strange Creatures Who Stopped Living and Became Mixed-Up Zombies* (1964), advertised as the "first monster musical". Unfortunately, the best thing about these movies is their titles – *Jesse James Meets Frankenstein's Daughter* looks like a cheap television western, for example.

A ridiculous premise is often enough for a film to be promoted as bad. Thus we have movies like *From Hell It Came* (1957), where a falsely accused man threatens revenge from beyond the grave just before he is killed. He is handily reincarnated as a tree. Or there's the self-explanatory equally silly *They Saved Hitler's Brain* (1963) and the dull *Night of the Lepus* (1972), featuring the dull Stuart Whitman, the dull Janet Leigh and the immortal line "There's a herd of killer rabbits heading this way". Which is about as exciting as it got. Digging further back there's *The Terror of Tiny Town* (1938), a B-

RIGHT Maria Frankenstein experiments on Jesse James' best friend Hank, later to be renamed Ygor, in *Jesse James Meets Frankenstein's Daughter*.

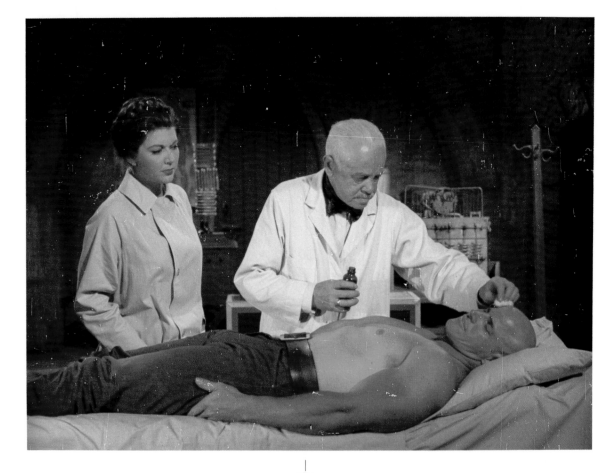

western whose only distinction is its all-midget cast.

There are far too many B-movie candidates to mention. Almost as much fun can be had watching an expensive disaster, like Irwin Allen's *The Swarm* (1978), which boasts a truly awful script by Stirling Silliphant. Richard Widmark was given more than his fair share of wretched dialogue as he battled the killer bees: "I always credit my enemy, no matter what he may be, with equal intelligence" and "General Thaddeus Slater is the first officer to get his butt kicked by a mess of bugs."

Finally, it has to be said that watching *Plan 9 From Outer Space* is a much better proposition than sitting through either *Auntie Mame* (1958) or Disney's *The Shaggy Dog* (1959), the two biggest money-earners in the year *Plan 9* was released. And it is infinitely preferable to that year's Best Picture Oscar winner, *Ben Hur* (1959). Perhaps our definition of "bad" needs reassessing.

ABOVE The vastly inferior remake of *King Kong* cost $24 million to produce.

LEFT Producer Irwin Allen spent vast amounts on Hollywood's biggest Bee-movie, *The Swarm*.

THE HARVARD LAMPOON'S AWARDS

The notion of movie worst awards stretches back much further than the late seventies. The *Harvard Lampoon* first announced its annual awards in 1940, partly (as it stated in 1963) "to supply a tonic to cure the ballyhoo and inanity of the Academy Awards". Some of the more entertaining, or ludicrous, awards have been:

★ The Worst Discoveries of 1944 were Maria Montez, star of exotic fantasies, the solid Van Johnson and, amazingly, Frank Sinatra.

★ The Happiest Announcement of 1950 was Shirley Temple's retirement.

★ The Biggest Argument for Stricter Immigration in 1951 was awarded to Mario Lanza.

★ The Most Degrading Moment of 1953 was considered to be Charles Laughton being hit over the head with a shovel by Lou Costello in *Abbott and Costello Meet Captain Kidd*.

★ The Most Thoroughly Unsatisfying Ending of 1956 was rightfully Rock Hudson's recovery in Douglas Sirk's *All That Heaven Allows*.

★ The Arrested-development Oblation in 1963 was given to that adult actor who has displayed the lowest level of maturity, and was "always given to Jerry Lewis".

★ The Cellophane Figleaf (for false modesty), 1963, was awarded to Ann-Margret "for insisting that she is not oversexed".

★ The Please-Don't-Put-Us-Through-DeMille-Again-Award was introduced in 1964 to be awarded "to that movie of the past year which embodies the pretentions, extravagance and blundering ineffectiveness of the traditional Screen Spectacular". The first film to win was fittingly George Stevens' overblown and stolid *The Greatest Story Ever Told*.

★ The Piltdown Mandible of 1966 was to be "presented annually for the lamest explanation of scientifically improbable phenomena", and was shared between *Fantastic Voyage* and *The Bible*, in the latter "to the lone cow . . . who supplied an estimated 974 gallons of milk to all the animals on the Ark for 40 days and 40 nights".

★ The OK-Doc-Break-the-Arm-Again Award for 1967, "to the most flagrant example of miscasting", was shared by "Charlton Heston for portraying a human being in *Planet of the Apes*".

BOTTOM RIGHT
Charlton Heston portraying a human being in *Planet of the Apes*.

BELOW The *Harvard Lampoon* might have been unimpressed, but Sirk's *All That Heaven Allows* with Rock Hudson and Jane Wyman is among the fifties best melodramas.

★ The Timothy Cratchit Memorial Crutch of 1969 was awarded "to that personality who offers the lamest justification for unsavoury behaviour", and went to "President Richard Nixon, who screened the film *Marooned*, an epic of three spacemen lost in the great beyond, for apprehensive astronauts Armstrong, Collins and Young at a White House *Kultur-fest*".

★ The Victor Mature Award is presented "in memory of Victor Mature who was heard to ask Barabbas in *The Robe* 'Is this your first crucifixion?'" This award is given to the most embarrassing line of dialogue. In 1974 it was won by George Kennedy for "his astute remark in *Earthquake*. 'Earthquakes bring out the worst in people'".

★ A Worst Movie Worst Award was presented in 1979, as it was felt the awards had been running long enough, "for the Harvard Lampoon Worst Award of the past 40 years which exemplifies their smarmy, undignified and scattershot approach". It went to their 1955 Worst Movie Ever Award, which went to *Rebel without a Cause*. It had been described as a "movie without a plot, such a wholly cretinous model of mediocre movie-making that we didn't even bother to see it. To prevent the perpetration of further cinematic abominations, let's pray that lead actors (we use the word perhaps too loosely) Sal Mineo and James Dean meet untimely deaths."

LEFT Ann-Margaret co-stars with Elvis in *Viva Las Vegas*. She won the "Cellophane Figleaf" award (for false modesty) in 1963.

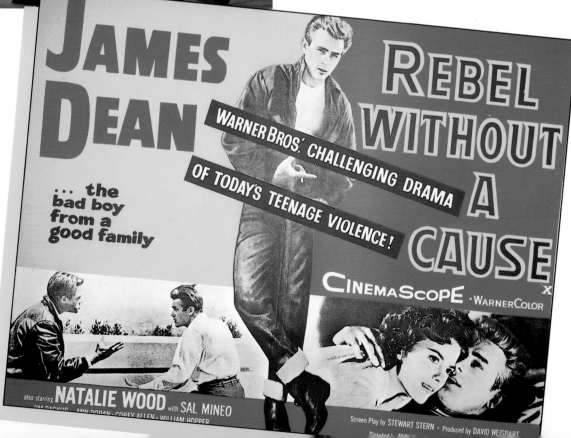

LEFT The *Harvard Lampoon* changed its opinion about *Rebel without a Cause* over 25 years awarding it the Worst Movie Worst Award.

INDEX

PICTURE CREDITS

The Publishers would like to thank the **Joel Finler Collection** for providing all of the pictures used in the book except for the following: pp36, 51: **Pictorial Press Limited**; pp43, 118, 120, 121: **BFI Stills, Posters and Designs**.

The publishers would also like to acknowledge the following film companies involved in the distribution and/or production of the films illustrated in the book, and apologize for any unintentional omissions:

ABC/John Foreman: Prizzi's Honour. **Columbia**: Lost Horizon, Mr Smith Goes to Washington, The Jolson Story, The Big Heat, It Happened One Night, The Lady from Shanghai. **Samuel Bronstein**: The Fall of the Roman Empire. **Carolco**: Terminator 2: Judgement Day. **Columbia/Delphi**: Ghostbusters. **Columbia/EMI**: Close Encounters of the Third Kind. **Columbia/IPC**: The China Syndrome. **Columbia/Stanley Jaffe**: Kramer vs Kramer **Columbia/Stanley Kramer**: Guess Who's Coming to Dinner? **Columbia/Mirage/Punch**: Tootsie. **Columbia/Rastar**: The Way We Were, Funny Girl. **Columbia/David Swift**: The Good Neighbour Sam. **Columbia/Sam Spiegel**: The Bridge on the River Kwai. **Embassy**: Jesse James Meets Frankestein's Daughter. **Epoch**: Birth of a Nation. **Fox**: Seventh Heaven, State Fair, Street Angel. **Gordon-Silver-Davis/TCF**: Predator. **Goscino**: The Battleship Potemkin. **Alfred Hitchcock**: Rear Window. **Samuel Goldwyn**: The Best Years of our Lives, The Little Foxes. **IFD/Romulus/Horizon**: The African Queen. **ITC/IPC**: On Golden Pond. **Stanley Kramer**: High Noon. **La Nouvelle Edition Francaise**: La Regle du Jeu. **Dino de Laurentis**: King Kong (remake). **London Films**: Richard III. **MGM**: Big Parade, Ben-Hur, Gone with the Wind, The Wizard of Oz,

Strike up the Band, Min and Bill, Random Harvest, Boy's Town, Broadway Melody, Viva Las Vegas. **Marianne/Dino de Laurentis**: Barbarella. **Orion/Hemdale/Pacific Western**: The Terminator. **PDS/Enic**: Bicycle Thieves. **Papillon Partnership/Corona/General Production Co**: Papillon. **Paramount**: Love Story, Road to Bali, Pardners, Wings. **Paramount/Alfran**: The Godfather. **Paramount/Cecil B DeMille**: The Ten Commandments (1956). **Paramount/Don Simpson, Jerry Bruckheimer**: Top Gun, Beverley Hills Cop. **Paramount/Famous Players-Laskey**: The Ten Commandments (1923), The Covered Wagon. **Paramount/Alfred Hitchcock**: Vertigo. **Paramount/Long Road**: Chinatown. **Paramount/Lucasfilm**: Raiders of the Lost Ark. **Paramount/Robert Stigwood**: Saturday Night Fever. **Paramount/Robert Stigwood, Allan Carr**: Grease. **Paramount/Hal B Wallis**: Becket. **Paramount/Martin Worth**. **RKO**: Citizen Kane, King Kong. **RKO/Kenneth MacGowan**: Becky Sharp. **Republic**: The Sands of Iwo Jima. **David O Selznick**: Duel in the Sun. **TCF/APJAC**: Planet of the Apes. **TCF/Argyle**: The Sound of Music. **TCF/Campanile**: Butch Cassidy and the Sundance Kid. **TCF/Chenault**: Hello Dolly. **TCF**: Gentlemen Prefer Blondes, Cleopatra, Wabash Avenue, The Seven Year Itch. **Touchstone**: The Color of Money. **UA/EON**: Dr. No. **UA/EON/Dan JAQ**: Diamonds are Forever. **Universal International**: Thunder Bay. **UA/Miriasch**: Some Like it Hot. **UA/Michael Cimino**: Heaven's Gate. **UA/Chartoff-Winkler**: Rocky. **Universal**: E.T. **Universal Elektra Film**: Extase. **Universal/Ross Hunter**: Airport. **Universal/Zanuck-Brown**: Jaws. **William J Reynolds**: Plan 9 from Outer Space. **TCF/Aspen**: M*A*S*H **Walter Wanger**: Joan of Arc. **Warner Bros**: The Singing Fool, Calamity Jane, On Moonlight Day, Rebel Without a Cause, The Swarm, The Jazz Singer, Lights of New York, Exorcist II: The Heretic, Batman. **Warner/Alexander Salkind**: Superman. **Warner/Amblin**: The Color Purple. **Warner/Hoya**: The Exorcist.